Fourteen Families
in Pueblo Pottery

Fourteen Families in Pueblo Pottery

Rick Dillingham
Foreword by J. J. Brody

University of New Mexico Press
Albuquerque

Library of Congress-in-Publication Data
Dillingham, Rick.
     Fourteen families in Pueblo pottery / Rick Dillingham; foreword by J.J. Brody.—1st ed.
          p. cm
Rev. and expanded ed. of: Seven families in Pueblo pottery, 1974.
ISBN 0-8263-1498-8.   ISBN 0-8263-1499-6 (pbk).
1. Pueblo Indians—-Pottery.
2. Pottery—Southwest, New.
I. Seven families in Pueblo pottery.
II. Title.
E99.P9D54   1994
738'.92'279—dc20
[B]
93-28021
     CIP
Copyright © 1994 by the University of New Mexico Press.

First edition

Editor: Dana Asbury
Charts: Carol Cooperrider
Color photographs: Herbert Lotz
Design: Mary Shapiro

Printed in Hong Kong

(page 1) *Aerial view of (left) Hano Pueblo and (right) Sichomovi Pueblo, Hopi, Arizona, 1948. Photo by Cutter-Carr Flying Service, courtesy Museum of New Mexico, negative number 2605.* **(page 81)** *Acoma Pueblo, ca. 1935. Photo by T. Harmon Parkhurst, courtesy Museum of New Mexico, negative number 2050.* **(page 105)** *Zia Pueblo, ca. 1935. Photo by T. Harmon Parkhurst, courtesy Museum of New Mexico, negative number 45998.* **(page 119)** *Cochiti Pueblo, ca. 1905. Courtesy Museum of New Mexico, negative number 82570.* **(page 128)** *Santo Domingo Pueblo, ca. 1935. Photo by T. Harmon Parkhurst, courtesy Museum of New Mexico, negative number 4367.* **(page 144)** *Pottery vendors, Santa Clara Pueblo, ca. 1935. Photo by T. Harmon Parkhurst, courtesy Museum of New Mexico, negative number 4212.* **(page 239)** *San Ildefonso Pueblo, ca. 1925. Photo by T. Harmon Parkhurst, courtesy Museum of New Mexico, negative number 3810.*

This book is dedicated to those potters who have left a legacy for the world to enjoy. I especially want to acknowledge the friendships developed with Helen Naha (the Feather Woman) and Alma Tahbo, who both passed away while this book was being written.

Contents

Acknowledgments

Without the help and patience of the potters involved, this book would not have been possible. I am fortunate to have gotten to know many of these potters over the past twenty years or so and was happy to meet new potters on this project. Many of these potters bent over backward to help me by assembling family members to visit with me on my sojourns to the pueblos. To them I am deeply indebted. My hope was that this would be a fun project for many of these families, and I think it was successful in this respect. I am grateful to those potters who loaned me pottery and helped me locate photos of older or deceased members of their families. All pottery and photos are credited in the book. I also thank those potters whom I constantly bothered with visits and phone calls to make sure I had all the descendants in proper order. I especially wish to thank Gilbert Atencio from San Ildefonso for preparing a chart of his family. Even after checking and rechecking, I apologize if some family members are still misplaced in the genealogies.

I also wish to thank Ray and Judy Dewey and Dee Ann Menuez of Dewey Galleries, Ltd., in Santa Fe for access to their inventory. Andrea Fisher and Robb Lucas of the Case Trading Post at the Wheelwright Museum were very generous in loaning items from the inventory. Andrea Fisher in her new shop, Fisher Fine Pottery, also loaned to the book. Ron McGee and Brent McGee of McGee's Trading Post in Keams Canyon, Arizona, helped me find pottery by potters I had not met or had trouble locating; their assistance was most valuable. Also generous with their inventories were Bob Andrews of Andrews Pueblo Pottery and Alexander Anthony and Rob Perry of the Adobe Gallery, both in Old Town Albuquerque, and Anthony Whitman of Otowi Trading Company, Santa Fe. Richard Cannon of Packard's Indian Trading Company in Santa Fe purchased much of what is credited "Rick Dillingham inventory." His generosity here enabled me to acquire many pots, saving much time in the photographing and documenting. Rita Neal of the Old Territorial Shop in Scottsdale, Arizona, shipped me an important piece to complete the Chapella family section. Paul Speckled Rock of Merrock Galeria in Santa Clara Pueblo gave generously of his time and inventory and was very helpful in introducing me to new potters. Kenneth Tafoya of the Jemu Povi Gallery introduced me to members of his family and always pointed me in the right direction. Thanks also to Richard Myers of Agape Southwest Pueblo Pottery in Albuquerque and the Santa Fe Indian Trading Company in Santa Fe.

At institutions in Santa Fe, I wish to thank Michael J. Hering and Christy Hoffman of the Indian Arts Research Center at the School of American Research for access to the collections. Bruce Bernstein of the Museum of Indian Art and Culture/Laboratory of Anthropology went out of his way to assist me on short notice, and Jonathan Batkin of the Wheelwright Museum was also generous with his time.

It is always a pleasure to work with private collectors willing to open their homes. Among those who contributed to this project are George Buckner and Jay Lazarus, New York City; James and Barbara Kramer, Santa Fe; Jim Vigil, Jemez Pueblo; and Joe Accardo and Maureen McCarthy, Santa Fe. The many potters who loaned works from their personal collections are listed in the photo credits.

A very special note of thanks goes to photographer Herb Lotz for his patience and consistency throughout the preparation of this book. When pots became available, I needed shots done quickly so I could return the pieces to their owners. Herb's flexibility and professionalism with this project were much appreciated.

Joan O'Donnell, director of the School of American Research Press, who worked wonders with my *Acoma and Laguna Pottery* book published by that press, put in personal time to help me edit this text and the potters' comments. Thank you once again.

When I first called Beth Hadas, director of the University of New Mexico Press, about updating and expanding the *Seven Families in Pueblo Pottery* book, she was very enthusiastic and came to visit me immediately. Her support and enthusiasm never flagged throughout the course of the project. I thank her for giving me the opportunity to complete a project very dear to my heart.

I had an initial idea of how the book should look and be designed. My ideal was created better than I had imagined by Mary Shapiro, who has done an exceptional job. She shows great sensitivity in her design and has elevated the book to the status of a beautiful object. I thank her for her collaboration and wonderful effort.

Carol Cooperrider is responsible for making the genealogies legible, and this was no easy task. I thank her for her patience and perseverance with this project. I wish also to thank my personal assistant, Juliette Myers, for her help with details of this project and for putting up with me.

In May of 1974, the "Seven Families in Pueblo Pottery" exhibit opened at the Maxwell Museum of Anthropology at the University of New Mexico in Albuquerque. The show and its modest accompanying catalogue created a great deal of interest in Pueblo pottery and launched the careers of many potters who still enjoy that recognition today.

The show's opening was an event that can never be repeated. Potters, many of them now deceased, came from all over pueblo country, bringing their families to celebrate, to renew old friendships, and to forge new ones. To an avid collector like myself, the event—full of potters and suffused with goodwill—was magic.

The simple catalogue for the exhibit, its cover originally adorned with only a Frank Stella-like "7," became a guide to anyone interested in collecting Pueblo pottery. (The current version, still in print, has the work of Hopi/Tewa potter Dextra Quotskuyva Nampeyo on the cover.) Originally released by the Maxwell Museum, the catalogue was later published by the University of New Mexico Press; some 80,000 copies are currently in print. As one of a few books then available on the subject, the catalogue was unexpectedly influential. One of its flaws was that it did not include as many families of exceptional potters as I could have presented. Some of these families are included in this updated and expanded volume. But even here, many families from various pueblos are missing.

The original "Seven Families" exhibition had its roots in my own pottery collection. I found I was attracted to pottery that was done within certain families and in similar styles. It is interesting to note that some families are "destined" somehow to be creative and others have individuals that may excel in art. Those selections were purely personal, as are the selections in this new publication. I make no value judgments about the talents and skills of the individual potters or the relative importance of the different families. The selections are based on my personal tastes, my friendships with the potters, and the potters' desire to work with me to present their families in this publication.

Another flaw of the original "Seven Families" book was that it was *too* influential: some beginning collectors felt that if a potter wasn't in the catalogue his or her work wasn't "collectable." Nothing could be further from the truth. There are exceptionally talented potters everywhere, many of them not connected to "dynasties" of potters like those represented here. The main criteria for including potters in these books is that they belong to families in which at least three generations have been active potters and/or painters. Many noted potters from all pueblos work alone or with only one other member of their family. These potters unfortunately are not included in this book.

Pottery has changed a good deal since 1974. Attitudes about traditions and innovations among potters have changed, and so have the collectors. The buyers of Pueblo pottery today are mainly non-Indian collectors, and today's work is tailored to this market. Since the 1970s, collectors have increasingly sought specific pieces, which they would commission from potters, to round out their collections. Working

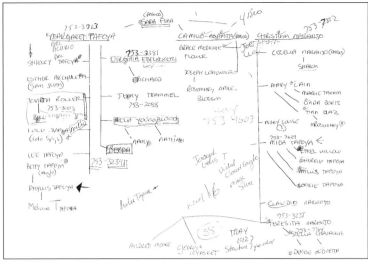

Top left: Opening day of the "Seven Families" exhibition at the Maxwell Museum of Anthropology, University of New Mexico, May 12, 1974. Left to right: Dextra Quotskuyva Nampeyo, Rachel Namingha Nampeyo, and Nellie Douma Nampeyo. Photo by Dick Dunatchik.

Top right: Original working drawing of part of the Tafoya family's genealogy, Santa Clara Pueblo, 1973–74.

Bottom: Four plaques from the original "Seven Families" exhibition at the Maxwell Museum of Anthropology in 1974. The potters made these pieces as nameplates for the cases that displayed their work (approximately 4 x 8 in.).

You are cordially invited
to the opening reception of

Families in Pueblo Pottery

a unique exhibition of contemporary pueblo pottery

May 12, 1974   11:30-5   Refreshments

Pottery demonstrations by Mary Cain and Christina Naranjo of Santa Clara Pueblo
Maxwell Museum of Anthropology, The University of New Mexico

Top left: Opening day of the "Seven Families" exhibition, Maxwell Museum of Anthropology, May 12, 1974. Left to right, top row: daughter of Emma Lewis Mitchell, Emma Lewis Mitchell, Delores Lewis Garcia, Carmel Lewis Haskaya, Rick Dillingham, unknown; bottom row: Clara Montoya, Maria Martinez, Lucy M. Lewis, Bernice Jones, unknown, Santana Martinez. Photo by Dick Dunatchik.

Bottom: Invitation to the original "Seven Families" exhibition, 1974.

Opposite: Mary Cain (left) and Christina Naranjo demonstrating at the opening of the "Seven Families" exhibition, May 12, 1974. Photographer unknown, courtesy of Mary Cain.

to order—to supply this growing market and earn a living—began cutting into potters' individual creativity. Some potters, then and now, resented these market pressures. Others have adapted their work to fit the market and have made strong commercial contributions.

The Indian art market is strong today, and creativity is blossoming all over the Pueblo world. Some potters, pushing the limits of a tradition they feel is antiquated, are making bold contemporary statements in clay. But tradition flourishes as well and has room for many individual creative statements. Many potters, deeply committed to traditional styles and methods, see in the newer work an upsetting erosion of tradition. Some members of the Tafoya family from Santa Clara Pueblo have chosen not to participate in this publication in protest of today's trend toward kiln-fired pottery and the practice of some potters misrepresenting nontraditional pottery to the buyer. Their gesture is noble but will not halt the relentless march into the future that nontraditional pottery represents. The book would have served as a vehicle for their individual statements of their preference for working in the styles they do. Instead, they gave me a statement from all involved.

Tradition itself is constantly being reinvented in Pueblo pottery. The distinctive carved pottery of Santa Clara and San Ildefonso was first made as recently as the 1920s. The sgraffito technique (sometimes erroneously termed "etched"—true etching involves an acid) is old to pottery in other parts of the world but very new to Pueblo pottery, begun by Popovi-Da and Tony Da at San Ildefonso in the mid- to late 1960s and carried to a pinnacle by Joseph Lonewolf and his family in the very early 1970s. In the 1990s potters from virtually every pueblo employ the sgraffito technique, and it is especially popular at Santa Clara. Using the technique on their slip-cast ware, Jemez, San Ildefonso, Acoma, and Laguna potters have created a whole new tourist market.

The black-on-black pottery made popular by Maria and Julian Martinez of San Ildefonso Pueblo was first made in the late teens of this century. The storyteller figures of Cochiti, though related to a figurative tradition of the latter part of the 1800s, were not made until the 1960s—spearheaded by Helen Cordero.

Hopi, Hopi/Tewa, and Zia potters like those in this book have carried on traditions that began centuries ago in their villages. But as commercialism becomes more prevalent in these villages, styles and tastes may change. Acoma Pueblo still keeps old stylistic traditions alive, but the electric kiln has all but supplanted the traditional outdoor sheep-manure firing.

The function of pottery has changed too—once made to be of practical use, it is now perceived as an art object. Service pottery and ceremonial pottery for personal and village use continue to be made today, and pottery is still traded among the pueblos as it has been for centuries. The difference in today's pottery manufacture is the Anglo desire to own unique and exceptional pieces. This has created divisions among potters and collectors alike.

We all—potter and collector alike—live in the late twentieth century, and I believe that to force Native American potters to remain, stylistically and technically, in the past is both unrealistic and patronizing. Traditional pottery may always have a solid place in the market and in Pueblo life, but as lifestyles change it also may be perceived by some as a limitation on innovation and individuality. Contemporary Native American artists may choose the less conservative path, pursuing their talent without worrying if their work will be accepted in the marketplace. Others value an anchor to the past, welcoming the continuity and timeless quality of traditional pottery. In the world of Pueblo pottery there seems to be room for both.

My interest in Pueblo pottery goes back to my early teens, as does my interest in ceramic art in general. Along with collecting and studying Pueblo pottery, I became a potter myself. This interest in collecting Indian pottery and learning ceramic art myself happened at roughly the same time. The quality of Pueblo pottery intrigued me because of its lack of slick technology. All the information came from the earth, as I hope my work conveys today. There is much more to clay than "mud." The clay, Mother Earth, is the vehicle that conveys potters' souls and is the glue that binds deep and lasting friendships. It is a tangible spiritual connection to life itself, and is not to be taken lightly. The clay is a great teacher, and many potters find joy in molding Mother Earth, listening to what She has to say, and attaining a center of peace while working. I have been very fortunate to know as many potters as I have, both Anglo and Native American. We all share a common ground.

Rick Dillingham
Santa Fe
June 1993

Foreword

The book you hold has its origins in a similar volume called *Seven Families in Pueblo Pottery*, which was originally published in 1974 by the Maxwell Museum of Anthropology as the catalogue of an exhibition of the same name; what you are reading now is as much an epilogue to the original as an introduction to its greatly expanded sequel. Though I worked at the Maxwell for many years before becoming its director in 1974, I can claim no credit for any part of *Seven Families*—neither the publication nor the exhibition which inspired it. Both came about when Professor John M. Campbell was its director and I was on leave, out of touch and out of the country. So I knew virtually nothing about either until the summer of 1974 and can talk about both as an almost disinterested party.

I have a first printing of *Seven Families* in front of me as I write this, and the credits listed on page 112 tell the initiated that almost the entire museum staff, including student employees such as Rick Dillingham and other part-time workers, contributed significantly to its creation. The staff was small and the project a corporate one produced by a talented group of people, most of whom simultaneously performed several different tasks. It is usual in such situations for those involved to lose track of their own contributions so that outsiders such as myself are entirely unable to credit individuals fairly for any particular part of the whole. The notion of "intellectual property" gets fuzzy around the edges, and the process is comparable in some ways to pottery making as it was, and sometimes still is, practiced by many of the extended families who were the subject of *Seven Families* as well as this book.

There is often a driving personality to these affairs, especially when the end product is strong and forceful, and in this instance Rick Dillingham appears to have filled that role. Rick was already an accomplished potter as well as a collector, student, and sometime dealer in Pueblo pottery. The exhibition and publication were largely his conception and shaped by his insights, which could well have been unique because of the many different ways in which he informed himself about Pueblo pottery and involved himself with it. It was a memorable show with a nicely complementary catalogue, and it took some time before I realized that we had a phenomenon on our hands.

Off-campus visitors kept coming, despite the frustrations of parking on the crowded campus of the University of New Mexico, and the catalogue kept selling, not only there, but also at Indian art and curio shops throughout the Southwest. I imagine we broke attendance records (for the most part we kept none in those days), and we certainly broke our catalogue sales records. Until then we had generally printed exhibition brochures or catalogues in editions of 2,000 or so, hoping to give away what did not sell only in the hundreds rather than the thousands. The first printing of *Seven Families* sold out, as did the second, and demand continued even after the exhibition closed. Having no desire to see the museum go into the book publishing business, I contracted with UNM Press to have them handle future printings which now number fifteen.

Phenomena occur with some regularity in the museum world and, like accidents, are defined by being unpredictable and explicable only after the fact, if at all. Why, for example, should one blockbuster exhibition about a historically obscure pharaoh named Tutankhamen play to great crowds, while another, equally well-produced and dramatizing with sex and violence the famed and sudden burial two millennia ago of Pompeii by volcanic ash, not excite the public imagination? Recognizing a phenomenon is not the same as understanding it, and periodically some of us speculated about *Seven Families* and why it had benefited from "the Tutankhamen effect." Its good title was certainly a factor, whose creator, though deserving of recognition, remains an anonymous member of that museum family. Timing was also important, and *Seven Families* was blessed by being sandwiched between the end of the family-commune–oriented hippie era, and the beginning of a burgeoning, worldwide interest in Native American art, life, and philosophy, which continues to this day. The reasons for that interest are many and varied and, in any case, can only have indirect bearing on the question for there have been many Pueblo pottery publications and exhibitions since, but few with its impact and longevity.

Title and timing tell only part of the story and then only if we look at what was novel about *Seven Families*. Its key innovation was the balance achieved between personal statements made by artists about their work and a focus on the cross-generational relationships between artists and their families. *Seven Families* projected the warm, personal qualities of the shared, corporate nature of creativity in the Pueblo world at the same time as it economically and effectively introduced many individual artists and their extended families to a wide audience. Those two themes of artist and community are greatly expanded in this new work, which also should intersect with a dynamic market for Pueblo pottery art in the outside world.

Euro-Americans have been collecting Pueblo Indian pottery in quantity since about 1880, but until the 1970s only two pottery artists, the Hopi-Tewa Nampeyo and Maria Martinez of San Ildefonso, had become at all well known to any but the most knowledgeable collectors. When large-scale collecting started, not only was most Pueblo pottery still made for household use rather than as something precious, but the notion of "pottery art" was almost as alien to the collectors as to the Pueblos. For the most part Pueblo potters and pottery painters were thought of as anonymous artisans producing useful and beautiful artifacts by conforming to prevailing community standards, and their works were interpreted as the products of particular places rather than the inventions of creative persons working within community traditions. Absence of signatures and other Euro-American markers of artistic individuality seemed only to confirm those judgments. By 1923, when Maria Martinez began systematically to sign her pottery, "pottery art" had become an established, if minor, fine art subcategory among Euro-Americans, and her work was thereafter accepted as a kind of art. But almost forty more years passed before most Pueblo pottery artists came to sign their works as a matter of course.

By the time of *Seven Families* most Pueblo pottery had long been made as a kind of art object for a non-Pueblo audience. Pots were essentially nonutilitarian, signed by their makers, and had come to signify—for many artists as well as their audience—both the creative individuality of an artist and the corporate values of the Pueblo communities within which they were made. That duality was perceived of only dimly then, for it was not often articulated and even now seems to be self-contradictory. Pueblo pottery traditions had changed markedly in almost every way imaginable since 1880, as had the Pueblos themselves, yet both somehow maintained their integrity and keen, creative relationships with the past. The new forms and traditions had dignity and seemed appropriate.

In 1974, Rick Dillingham—artist, student, scholar, collector, dealer—was led both by an ethical imperative and by the conviction of positive, practical market consequences to conceive of an exhibition and book that would give Pueblo pottery artists opportunity to be seen in equal part as creative individuals and as members of traditional communities. The *Seven Families* phenomenon was the result, and credit the Maxwell Museum and Jack Campbell and his staff as well as Dillingham for shaping the concept into a reality. Twenty years later, we have another imperative, another reality, and another book twice the size. Twenty years from now, we'll see.

J. J. Brody
September 1993

Subsistence

In the early seventies
I lived at Kha Po̅ʹo O̅wengé*
with my Grandparents.
I sometimes stayed with my great Grandmother, Gía Kwijo̅,
who was a potter.
She taught me to make small pots and figurines
and we sold them to the tourists.
When we worked with the clay
it would dry on my hands, and
when I peeled it off
there were small white patches
where it had bleached my skin.
After a few minutes
my darker colored flesh returned;
it was the clay that showed me
who I really was.

Years have passed since Gía Kwijo̅ died.
I still remember the strength of her hands
as she taught me
to shape the clay.
And I often wonder
about those small pots and figurines;
who bought them and
where they are now.
Sometimes I see Gía Kwijo̅'s reflection
in the pots she made
that now sit
on my Grandparents' mantel.
It reminds me
that like all the women in my family, and
all things at Kha Po̅ʹo O̅wengé,
I am made of clay, too.

RoseMary Diaz

*Original Tewa name for Santa Clara Pueblo

About the Photographs

All portraiture was done by Rick Dillingham unless otherwise noted. Photographs of deceased potters or of individuals who were away at the times I was photographing were borrowed from family members, rephotographed by Herbert Lotz, and cropped to fit this book. In some cases I was unable to schedule photo sessions and no existing portraits were available; these potters are not pictured here. A very few potters preferred not to be photographed.

All color photographs of the pottery in this book were taken by Herbert Lotz. The pieces pictured are from my personal collection, from other private collections both in the Southwest and across the country, from the potters' homes, and from stores, galleries, and museums.

Key to captions: The name of each potter is followed by the dimensions of the pictured pot (height x diameter), its date of manufacture, and its source.

About the Genealogy Charts

The charts that appeared in the original *Seven Families in Pueblo Pottery* book were used as a starting point for this publication. They were amended where necessary, as new generations of potters working today were included. The members of the original seven families and the additional seven families in this new publication helped create and double-check the charts to ensure as correct a lineage as possible.

I regret that I could not include everyone in these family trees. I tried to focus on potters' relatives but had to stray now and then to make as complete a family tree as possible. Many people listed as painters were instrumental in pottery decoration and styling. I wanted to present as much detail as possible, so the genealogies in this book are far more complex than in the earlier *Seven Families*. Despite the checking and double-checking, however, I'm sure some individuals have been left out. I have tried to bring each family up to the present, and with any luck the young people listed in this book will be pleased to see their connection in the family of pottery in the future. Some adopted children are listed both with their natural parents and with the adults who raised them. In some cases, adopted children are not specifically noted and are listed as children of the adopting parents. The last names listed are those the potters or their family members are using at present. Names change, and I apologize for any errors in that area. Deceased family members are listed with a (d.) following their names. Potters are noted with color in the charts. If someone is a noted painter or other craftsperson, I have tried to make note of it.

Map of the Pueblos

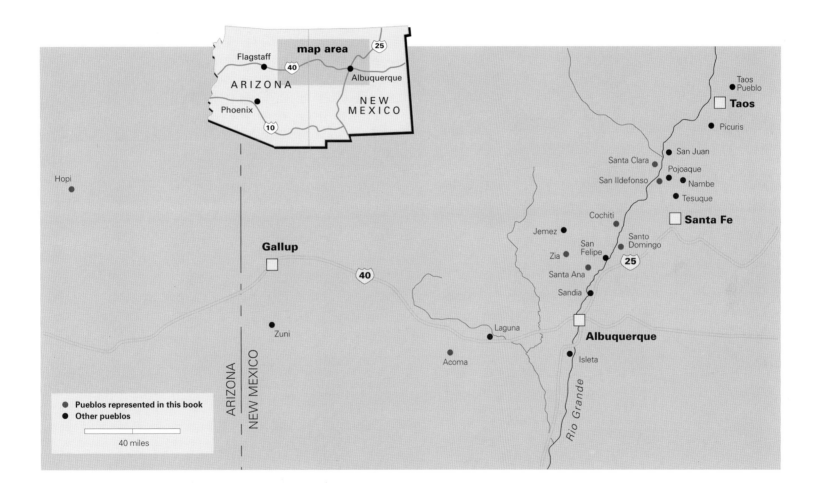

Flagstaff

map area

40

25

ARIZONA

Albuquerque

NEW MEXICO

Phoenix

10

Hopi

Gallup

40

Zuni

ARIZONA

NEW MEXICO

● Pueblos represented in this book
● Other pueblos

40 miles

Taos Pueblo

☐ Taos

Picuris

San Juan

Santa Clara

Pojoaque

San Ildefonso

Nambe

Tesuque

Cochiti

☐ Santa Fe

Jemez

Santo Domingo

Zia

San Felipe

25

Santa Ana

Sandia

Laguna

☐

Albuquerque

Acoma

Isleta

Rio Grande

HOPI-TEWA

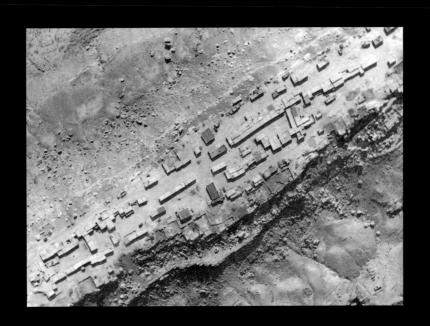

The Chapella Family

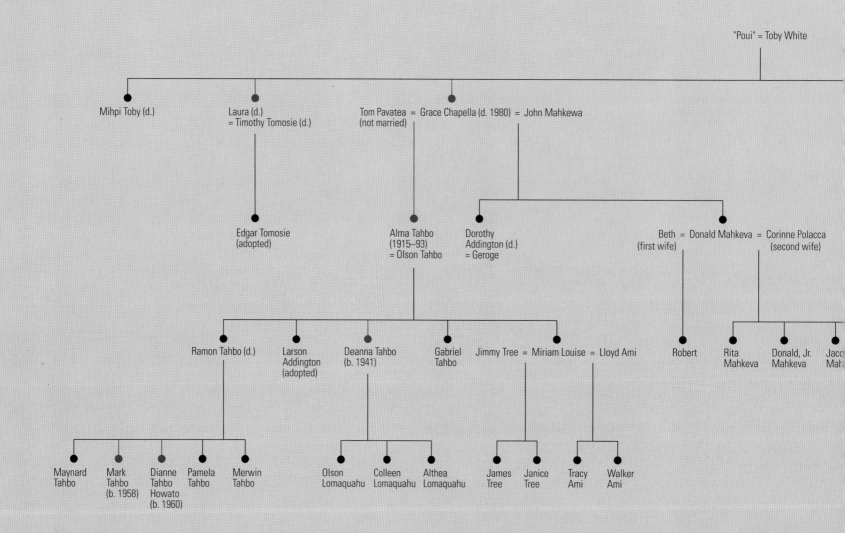

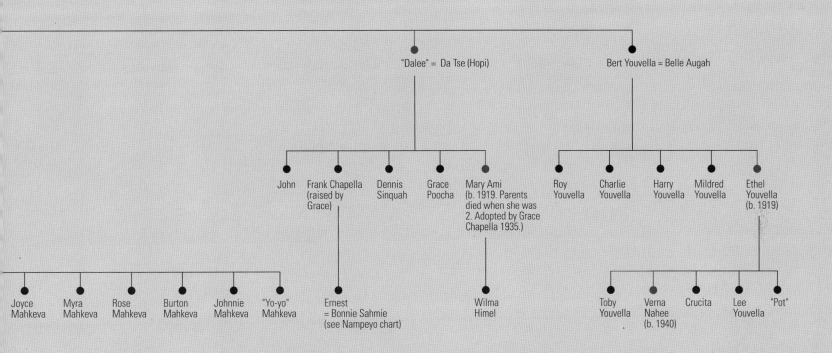

"Dalee" = Da Tse (Hopi) Bert Youvella = Belle Augah

John | Frank Chapella (raised by Grace) | Dennis Sinquah | Grace Poocha | Mary Ami (b. 1919. Parents died when she was 2. Adopted by Grace Chapella 1935.)

Roy Youvella | Charlie Youvella | Harry Youvella | Mildred Youvella | Ethel Youvella (b. 1919)

Joyce Mahkeva | Myra Mahkeva | Rose Mahkeva | Burton Mahkeva | Johnnie Mahkeva | "Yo-yo" Mahkeva

Ernest = Bonnie Sahmie (see Nampeyo chart)

Wilma Himel

Toby Youvella | Verna Nahee (b. 1940) | Crucita | Lee Youvella | "Pot"

Opposite: Laura Tomosie (portrait not available). Pot 6 ¼ x 9 in., ca. 1965. Courtesy Old Territorial Shop, Scottsdale, Arizona.

Grace Chapella, ca. 1974 (photograph by Glenn Short). Pot 10 x 17 in., ca. 1955. Rick Dillingham collection.

Alma Tahbo, b. 1915
"I learned from my mother [Grace Chapella]. I used to just play with her pottery and make all kinds of things, then I started to make larger [pottery]. My mother took over these children of Dahlee: Frank, John, Dennis, Mary [Ami], and Grace. She had a hard time and started to work at Polacca Day School as a cook and a housekeeper. We were all raised with grandmother "Povi" Toby. In 1983 I had a stroke and was still making pottery up to then. The second stroke in 1986 really got me down.

All you think of is your pottery work. You don't care about cleaning the house. If you worried about other things when the pots were being fired, they would crack."

Deanna Tahbo, b. 1941
*"I kind of just watched
Grandma [Grace Cha-
pella], and I started
molding little pieces,
and as the years went
by I added on and
made bigger pottery.
I give my credit for
inspiration to her."*

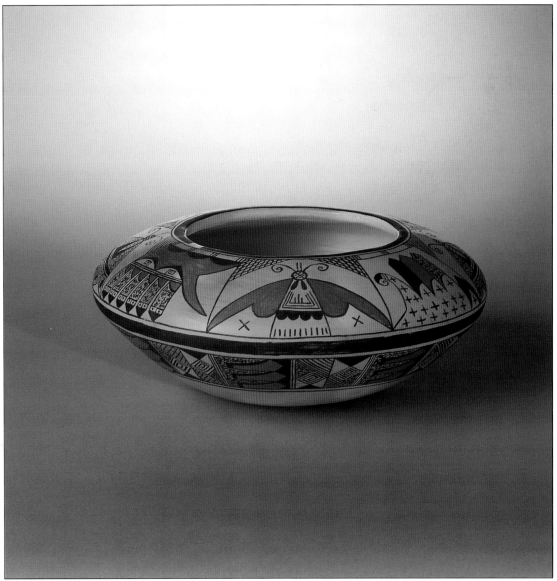

*Opposite: Alma Tahbo. Pot 7 ½ x 11
in., 1981. Rick Dillingham collection.*

*Deanna Tahbo. Pot 4 ½ x 10 ½ in.,
1986. Rick Dillingham collection.*

Mark Tahbo, b. 1958
"Grace [Chapella] was really a unique person. She was something special, and I've always admired her. She was a great inspiration to me. She was pretty old when I got interested [in pottery making], and she couldn't really give me all I needed to know. She was maybe 100, and her mind had slipped, so most was self-taught. I went through mistakes and errors. My pots today have a lot more 'being' than just a pot. To me they have life and sensitivity, just like a human being. When I create a pot I breathe life into it and hope it lives."

Dianna Tahbo Howato, b. 1960
"I consider the background of where [pottery making] came from, the family. I learned from observing. I learned most of what I know from Mark [Tahbo]. I was always interested in it since I first noticed pottery, and I got a lot of good feedback from Mark. I've grown to learn that pottery becomes a part of you . . . the feelings of that, and how I identify with it and how it identifies with me."

Top: Mark Tahbo. Pot 4 x 11 ¾ in., 1991. Rick Dillingham collection.

Bottom: Dianna Tahbo Howato. Pot 4 ½ x 7 in., 1991. Rick Dillingham collection.

Opposite: "Dalee" (portrait not available). Pot (identified by Grace Chapella, ca. 1972) 2 ½ x 4 ¾ in., ca. 1920s. Rick Dillingham collection.

Mary Ami, b. 1919
Mary Ami's mother, "Dahlee," died when Mary
was two years old. She was raised by Grace
Chapella, who then became her "mother."

*"When I was real little, I did the pottery with my
grandma (Grace and my mom's mother), and I
started pounding out pots on my elbow. Before I
got married (in 1945), I worked with my mother
[Grace]. Dahlee was living at the Bear House next
door to Nampeyo. She [Nampeyo] told me that
they worked together and Dahlee told her how to
make pottery. Nampeyo took care of me as a baby.
My grandmother worked with Nampeyo."*

Mary Ami signed her pottery "Mary Ami" until she
got married. She said that she changed the signa-
ture to "Buffalo Maiden" at the request of an uncle.

Verna Nahee, b. 1940
"I like working with both types of the clay, red and gray [yellow]. With red I mainly do corrugated types. I enjoy making pottery. It means a lot. It gives me a good feeling when I work with clay. My mom learned from Grace Sayah [sayah is Tewa for grandmother] [Chapella], and I learned from both she and my mother. When we fire like this we think back on how she [Grace] did it. Ours is kind of 'broader' in design, others do finer designs. Making pottery isn't an easy thing. You have to have a clear mind. You have to be in the mood or they won't turn out. I like just to make to satisfy me. I don't take orders. To me taking orders is to satisfy someone else, and they never come out right."

Ethel Youvella, b. 1919
"I learned some from my mother's mother, Lela. I would mold little ones and she would fix them up for me. I used to go down to do pottery with Grace [Chapella] and Laura [Tomosie]. I learned to fire the red ones from Grace. I didn't get them to come out right until she helped. I didn't know how to do it [red pottery], so I did it her way and learned. If the paint doesn't stick I go over it and refire it. I hate to be selling it without the paint being right. Some tourists don't care, but I don't want to sell it that way."

Opposite: Verna Nahee. Pot 5 x 9 in., ca. 1980. Courtesy James and Barbara Kramer, Santa Fe.

Ethel Youvella. Pot 3 ½ x 4 in., ca. 1980. Courtesy James and Barbara Kramer, Santa Fe.

The Nampeyo Family

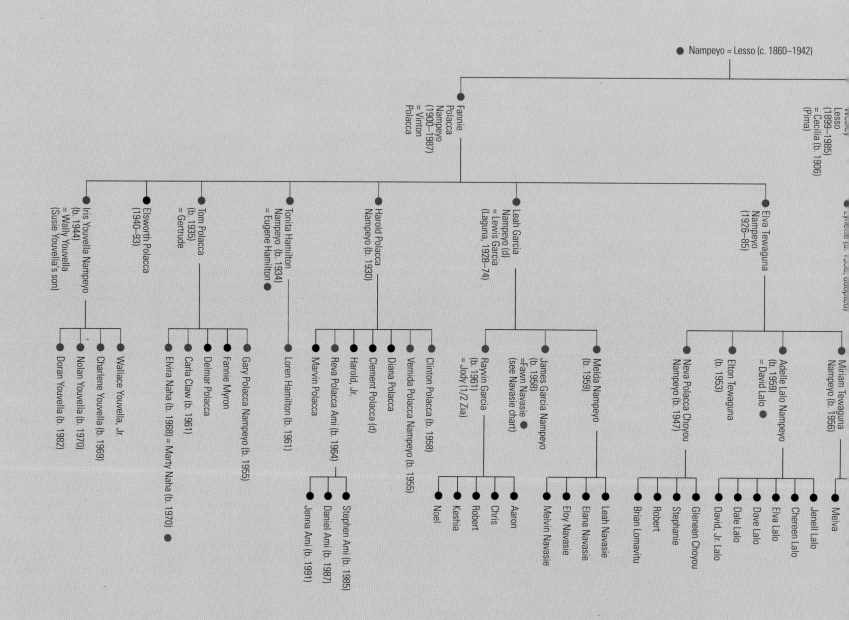

Nampeyo = Lesso (c. 1860–1942)

(Wesley)
Lesso
(1899–1985)
= Cecilia (b. 1906)
(Pima)

Fannie
Polacca
Nampeyo
(1900–1987)
= Vinton
Polacca

Iris Youvella Nampeyo
(b. 1944)
= Wally Youvella
(Susie Youvella's son)

Elsworth Polacca
(1940–93)

Tom Polacca
(b. 1935)
= Gertrude

Tonita Hamilton
Nampeyo (b. 1934)
= Eugene Hamilton

Harold Polacca
Nampeyo (b. 1930)

Leah Garcia
Nampeyo (d.)
= Lewis Garcia
(Laguna, 1928–74)

Elva Tewaguna
Nampeyo
(1926–85)

Lyncito (b. 1908; stepson)

Miriam Tewaguna
Nampeyo (b. 1956)

Doran Youvella (b. 1982)

Nolan Youvella (b. 1970)

Charlene Youvella (b. 1969)

Wallace Youvella, Jr.

Elvira Naha (b. 1968) = Marty Naha (b. 1970)

Carla Claw (b. 1961)

Delmar Polacca

Fannie Myron

Gary Polacca Nampeyo (b. 1955)

Loren Hamilton (b. 1961)

Marvin Polacca

Reva Polacca Ami (b. 1964)

Harold, Jr.

Clement Polacca (d)

Diana Polacca

Vernida Polacca Nampeyo (b. 1955)

Clinton Polacca (b. 1958)

Rayvin Garcia
(b. 1961)
= Jody (1/2 Zia)

James Garcia Nampeyo
(b. 1958)
= Fawn Navasie
(see Navasie chart)

Melda Nampeyo
(b. 1959)

Neva Polacca Choyou
Nampeyo (b. 1947)

Elton Tewaguna
(b. 1953)

Adelle Lalo Nampeyo
(b. 1959)
= David Lalo

Jenna Ami (b. 1991)

Daniel Ami (b. 1987)

Stephen Ami (b. 1985)

Noel

Keshia

Robert

Chris

Aaron

Melvin Navasie

Eloy Navasie

Elana Navasie

Leah Navasie

Brian Lomavitu

Robert

Stephanie

Gleneen Choyou

David, Jr. Lalo

Dale Lalo

Dave Lalo

Elva Lalo

Chereen Lalo

Jenell Lalo

Melva

14

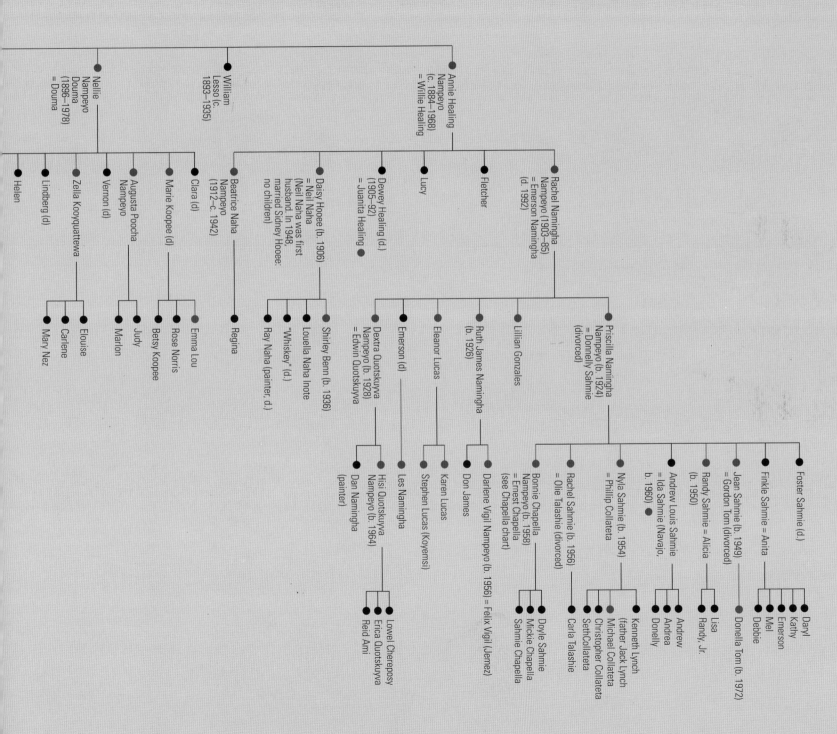

Annie Healing
(c. 1884–1968)
= Willie Healing

William
Lesso (c.
1893–1935)

Nellie
Nampeyo
Douma
(1896–1978)
= Douma

Rachel Namingha
Nampeyo (1903–85)
= Emerson Namingha
(d. 1992)

Fletcher

Lucy

Dewey Healing (d.)
(1905–92)
= Juanita Healing ●

Daisy Hooee (b. 1906)
= Neil Naha
(Neil Naha was first
husband. In 1948,
married Sidney Hooee:
no children)

Beatrice Naha
Nampeyo
(1912–c. 1942)

Clara (d)

Marie Koopee (d)

Augusta Poocha
Nampeyo

Vernon (d)

Zella Kooyquattewa

Lindberg (d)

Helen

Regina

Ray Naha (painter, d.)

"Whiskey" (d.)

Louella Naha Inote

Shirley Benn (b. 1936)

Emma Lou

Rose Norris

Betsy Koopee

Judy

Marlon

Elouise

Carlene

Mary Nez

Dextra Quotskuyva
Nampeyo (b. 1928)
= Edwin Quotskuyva

Emerson (d.)

Eleanor Lucas

Ruth James Namingha
(b. 1926)

Lillian Gonzales

Priscilla Namingha
Nampeyo (b. 1924)
= Donnelly Sahmie
(divorced)

Hisi Quotskuyva
Nampeyo (b. 1964)

Les Namingha

Karen Lucas

Stephen Lucas (Koyemsi)

Don James

Darlene Vigil Nampeyo (b. 1956) = Felix Vigil (Jemez)

Bonnie Chapella
Nampeyo (b. 1958)
= Ernest Chapella
(see Chapella chart)

Rachel Sahmie (b. 1956)
= Olie Talashie (divorced)

Nyla Sahmie (b. 1954)
= Phillip Collateta

b. 1960) ●

Andrew Louis Sahmie
= Ida Sahmie (Navajo,

Randy Sahmie = Alicia
(b. 1950)

Jean Sahmie (b. 1949)
= Gordon Tom (divorced)

Finkle Sahmie = Anita

Foster Sahmie (d.)

Dan Namingha
(painter)

Reid Ami

Erica Quotskuyva

Lowel Chereposy

Doyle Sahmie

Mickie Chapella

Sahmie Chapella

Carla Talashie

Kenneth Lynch
(father Jack Lynch

Michael Collateta

Christopher Collateta

SethCollateta

Donelly

Andrea

Andrew

Randy, Jr.

Lisa

Donella Tom (b. 1972)

Debbie

Mel

Emerson

Kathy

Daryl

15

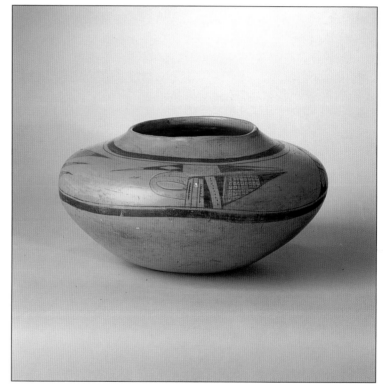

Nampeyo with her daughter Fannie (historic postcard, ca. 1930, courtesy Daisy Hooee). Pots: left: three-color polychrome, 5 x 10 ½ in., ca. 1900, Rick Dillingham collection; right: red-slipped polychrome, 8 x 15 in., ca. 1910–15; Rick Dillingham collection; opposite: white-slipped polychrome, 7 x 13 ½ in., ca. 1905, Rick Dillingham collection.

Tonita Hamilton Nampeyo, b. 1934
"I want to continue the traditional methods and designs. I don't want to deviate from what my mom [Fannie Polacca] and grandmother [Nampeyo] did and hand it down to the young ones. That's the most important thing, to keep tradition alive."

Opposite: Fannie Polacca Nampeyo, ca. 1972. Pot 7 x 11 in., ca. 1965. Rick Dillingham collection.

Tonita Hamilton Nampeyo. Pot 5 ½ x 3 ½ in., 1979. Rick Dillingham collection.

Eugene Hamilton
"I do some traditional, that's how I got in, and now I do the sgraffito, depending upon what mood I'm in."

Left: Eugene Hamilton. Pot 3 ¼ x 3 ½ in., 1992. Rick Dillingham inventory.

Right: Loren Hamilton. Pot 3 x 3 ½ in., 1992. Rick Dillingham inventory.

Opposite: Leah Garcia Nampeyo, ca. 1972. Pot 5 x 7 ¾ in., ca. 1965. Rick Dillingham collection.

Loren Hamilton, b. 1961
"[I learned] from being around the family, my grandmother [Fannie] and mom [Tonita]. I spent a year with Tom [Polacca] and learned from him. I started on my own and did the best I could. In the past year I started with sculpture, and a few months ago I started adding red slip.

"I strive to do my best and depict what we believe in on my pots. I try to take old designs and interpret them in my way. I've done it with moths and fine lines. I am working full time on potting now, and try to produce something people enjoy. As long as someone's happy, I'm happy."

Melda Navasie Nampeyo, b. 1959
"My grandma [Fannie Polacca] really told me to learn this. My little girls are starting to work on them, little pots, and they've sold a couple already. This is mostly the design I use, the black design. My mom [Leah Garcia] and grandmother painted for me. I've been working since 1985, I think, on my own."

Melda Nampeyo. Pot 3 x 3 ¼ in., 1992. Rick Dillingham inventory.

Opposite top: James Garcia Nampeyo. Pot 4 ½ x 9 in., 1992. Rick Dillingham inventory.

Opposite bottom: Rayvin Garcia. Pot 4 x 7 ½ in., 1992. Rick Dillingham inventory.

James Garcia
Nampeyo, b. 1958
"I carry on the tradition of Nampeyo and got started with my wife [Fawn]. My grandmother [Fannie] really got me started, and I used to have her work with me. I would mold them and she would paint them. Then she said I had to get going on my own, and I painted my first pot in front of her.

"All the designs I do are old traditional Nampeyo designs. I haven't tried anything new. Fawn molds some of the larger ones, and we work together. I do the smaller ones."

Rayvin Garcia, b. 1961
"I've been at it [pottery making] about nine years, since I've been married, and it's mainly my grandmother [Fannie Polacca] who taught me. I took her painting style, and I don't want to go into other designs. This is the best way of making a living for my family."

23

Iris Youvella Nampeyo, b. 1944
"When I was just a little girl I would sit by my mother [Fannie Polacca] mak-
ing little ladles, and I didn't know how to paint. My father said, 'Why don't you
paint a corn on the ladle?' [the Nampeyo family belongs to the Corn Clan]
and I thought he meant to build up a corn. Then I started painting, and then I
got back to the reservation and saw all the traditional pots. And then I saw a
pot with a corn on it and remembered what my dad said, and I thought I'd go
in that direction. It was a Navajo pot. I feel a closeness to the corn because of
my clan."

Iris Youvella Nampeyo. Pots: oppo-
site: 4 ½ x 6 in., 1992, courtesy
Otowi Trading Co., Santa Fe; right:
2 ¼ x 4 ½ in., ca. 1980, courtesy of
the artist.

Nolan Youvella, b. 1970
"I first started out when I was about eleven. I used to make little pipes. After a while I started making pottery. I work with carving pottery, and later on I'll want to try painting. I was going to school for one and a half years and then I came back and started up with pots again."

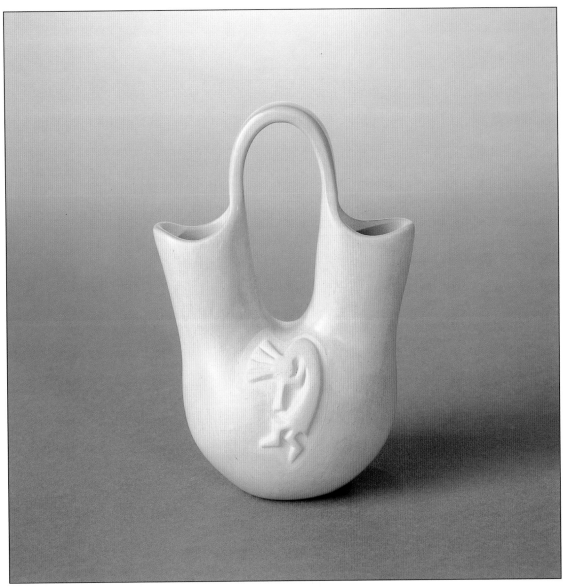

Nolan Youvella. Pot 5 x 3 ½ in., 1991. Courtesy Iris Youvella Nampeyo.

Opposite: Wallace Youvella (portrait not available). Pot 4 x 6 ¾ in., 1992. Courtesy McGees Indian Art, Keams Canyon, Arizona.

Charlene Youvella, b. 1969
"I would watch Fannie make pottery. I watched how she molded and fired. She gave me a chance to play with the clay she had, and that helped me to learn myself. I'll probably stay with miniatures. I've never tried painting. I'll stay with my mom's style. My dad helps me with them also."

Opposite: Wallace Youvella, Jr. (portrait not available). Pot 2 x 3 in., 1992. Courtesy Otowi Trading Co., Santa Fe.

Doran Youvella and Charlene Youvella. Doran Youvella pot 1 ¼ x 2 in., 1992, courtesy of the artist; Charlene Youvella pot ½ x 1 ¼ in., 1992, courtesy of the artist.

Vernida Nampeyo, b. 1955
"My pots, the pots I do, I only paint the fineline. I want to keep the tradition up, so I mainly stay with fineline. The main thing is keeping the tradition up. I fire the same way my Grandmother Fannie taught me. I do my baking [firing] in Polacca, not here in the canyon [Keams Canyon]. I worked with my dad [Harold Nampeyo] when he was well. He would make them and I would paint for him. I started learning how twelve years ago, and I learned all from Fannie.

"It means a lot to me to do painting. It's in a way like—it relaxes me—it's harmonious. Sometimes I'm not in the mood, and when I am the paint flows. If you're angry, lazy, your paint will fall off the pots. You have to want to do it and be in a good mood. Spiritually it helps you get going with pottery. It does bring in income, but I have another job on the side."

Opposite: Vernida Polacca Nampeyo. Pot 3 x 5 ½ in., 1992. Rick Dillingham inventory.

Harold Polacca Nampeyo (portrait not available). Pot painted by Fannie Nampeyo, 4 x 6 ½ in., ca. 1975. Rick Dillingham collection.

Reva Ami, b. 1964
"I learned mainly from Vernida [Nampeyo]. She's the one who kept pushing me to start. I've only been potting since last July—1 year. I talked with Tonita [Hamilton Nampeyo] and Adelle [Nampeyo] and they have helped me quite a lot. I like doing it [pottery]. It's interesting. I'm sticking to the family's designs and I'm trying to get back into the older ones like my grandmother [Fannie Nampeyo]. I don't look far in the future, but I want to start making larger ones."

Clinton Polacca, b. 1958
"I learned from watching my grandmother, Fannie. I just starting doing pots by myself four years ago. I used to just make them, and she'd paint them. I have a respect for the designs. I usually just sell to people who really want them and connect with the design and respect it."

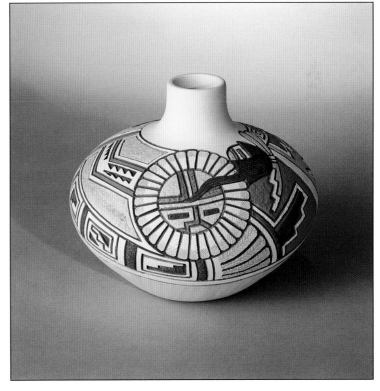

Opposite: Reva Polacca Ami. Pot 4 ⅞ x 9 in., 1993. Courtesy Merrock Galeria, Santa Clara Pueblo.

Left: Clinton Polacca. Pot 4 x 6 ¼ in., 1992. Rick Dillingham inventory.

Right: Tom Polacca Nampeyo (portrait not available). Pot 7 x 8 in., 1992. Rick Dillingham inventory.

Gary P. Nampeyo, b. 1955

"That style [carved pottery] was given to me by my father [Tom Polacca], and I've kind of come up with my own as well, different from his. I try to texture it with the scenery around here. If you look at rocks they're never all smooth. It gives the background a different look. The colors that go into it are similar to what surrounds us here at Hopi.

"I like to try to get across the ancientness of our people. That's what the style means to me. I try to tell a story with my pottery and use figures. Our people have been spread out across the Southwest with ruins, and when I use a flute player I try to bring back the past—what we see on pictographs.

"I use a carving knife—a kind of razor knife—and I use yucca paintbrushes and whatever I find to my liking."

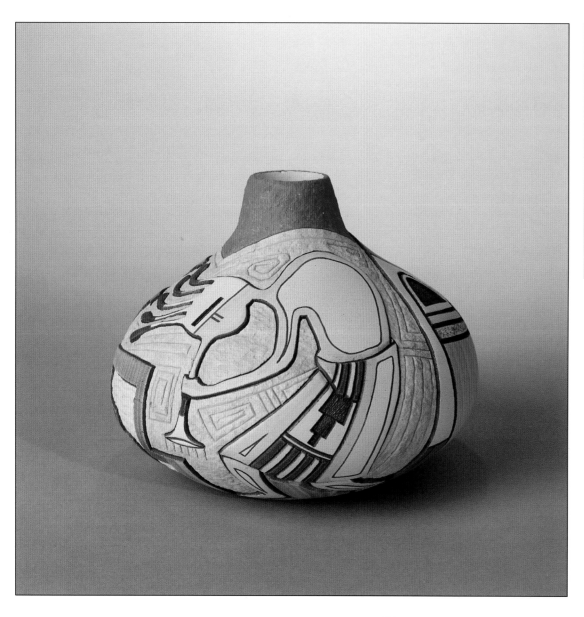

34

Elvira Naha b. 1968
"I just learned from my dad [Tom Polacca], and he told me to try and I did. It's just a style [sgraffito] I stay with now. I use mostly kachina designs on my pots. I use all natural materials but fire mostly in a kiln."

Marty Naha, b. 1970
"I learned it off of Tom [Polacca] and his daughter Elvira. She's the one who really got me into it. We've been doing this for about two and a half years now. It's good money and we make a living with it. Tom invented this style [sgraffito]."

Carla Claw, b. 1961
"Mainly my work is kind of different from everybody's. I use a dark brown polished slip on plain seed pots done with sgraffito carving like my dad [Tom Polacca] does. It's kind of unique in a way—to me it's modern. That's the outlook now. Things that are different are more accepted, but they're done in traditional form that links us back to who we are."

Opposite: Gary Polacca Nampeyo. Pot 6 x 7 ½ in., 1992. Rick Dillingham inventory.

Elvira Naha. Pot not available.

Carla Claw. Pot 2 ½ x 1 ¾ in., 1992. Rick Dillingham inventory.

Miriam Tewaguna Nampeyo, b. 1956
"I feel good about doing pottery. It's the only thing I do now. It excites me to work. It took me quite a while after I got out of high school, four or five years. Then my mom [Elva Tewaguna] really started teaching me the pottery. Then I started on my own, not painting right off, especially the 'fineline,' which was taught to me by my younger sister, Adelle."

Opposite: Elva Tewaguna Nampeyo, ca. 1972. Pot 6 ½ x 13 in., ca. 1980. Rick Dillingham collection.

Miriam Tewaguna Nampeyo. Pot 4 ½ x 5 in., 1992. Rick Dillingham inventory.

Adelle Lalo Nampeyo, b. 1959
Adelle's husband, David Lalo, has been potting in the carved style for two years.
"I guess I'm so glad I learned this from my mom [Elva Tewaguna] and grandma [Fannie Polacca], and now I'm trying to teach my girls. It means a lot to me to make pots, the spiritual way means a lot. I've tried some designs on my own but never really put it down on paper to continue them. I've tried them and let them go. I've stayed with designs in the family—fineline and black design [solid fineline or `migration pattern']."

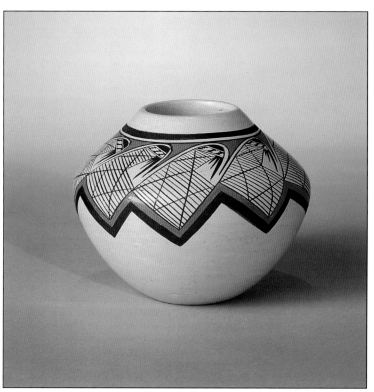

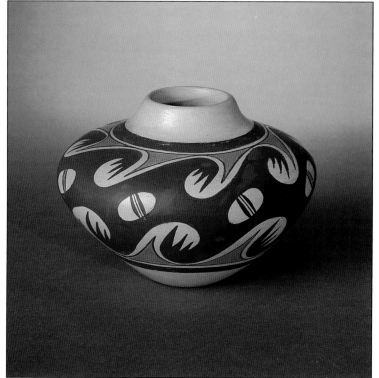

Left: Adelle Lalo Nampeyo. Pot 4 x 5 ¼ in., 1992. Rick Dillingham inventory.

Right: Neva Polacca Choyou Nampeyo (portrait not available). Pot 4 x 5 ⅜ in., ca. 1980. Courtesy James and Barbara Kramer, Santa Fe.

Opposite: Lynette Lesso. Two pots, each 3 ¼ in. tall, 1991. Courtesy of the artist.

Lynette Lesso, b. 1955
"My mom [Cecelia Lesso] told you in the first book that I would take over. She was my adopted mother, and she taught me so much that she learned from Nampeyo. She told me it would be a way to make a living, carrying it on.

"When I'm doing pottery I think good things. I let it go when there are ceremonies. I do all of it myself—clay, manure. I'm friends with some Navajos and they bring me the manure. From molding, sanding, polishing I do all of it myself. I teach my kids how to paint. I mix up designs—not in the order she [Cecelia] always used them.

"He [Wesley] helped my mom in gathering and in ideas with some of the designs, the manure, and clay. The rest she did on her own. He was there to back her up. When I'm doing this I think of my mom a lot."

39

Daisy Hooee, b. 1906

"My first husband was Neil Naha, and he left us
and I came to Zuni to see the `doings' [ceremonies]
to get happy. Then I got a job here cooking in
Ramah and worked with 4-H boys and girls, lots of
jobs. [She married Sidney Hooee, a Zuni in 1948;
her children are with Neil Naha.]

"I taught pottery at the high school [Zuni], and I made
it in the old way like my grandmother, Nampeyo. I
learned from Nampeyo and so did my mother, Annie.
Everybody painted for her—Nellie, Fannie, and my
mother helped her a lot, painted those little fine lines.
Rachel [Daisy's sister] painted for her, too. Her husband Lesso, he helped—he sure can paint, that old
man too. [Documented examples of Lesso's painting
are virtually nonexistent.] It was nice to have such
a kind grandmother. She would never say `Don't
bother the clay' when we wanted to make little
things.

"They [Daisy's mother and father] had sheep and
cows, and she [Annie] made pots too. She was a
busy woman. The Navajo herded sheep for us,
and she made all kinds of food, piki. She would
herd sheep herself, and Grandma Nampeyo
would come with her husband, and the old man
herded sheep while she [Annie] painted pots.

"Nampeyo had trouble with her voice as well as
her eyes, and at a point couldn't talk well, but she
could laugh!

"I appreciate everything I've learned from you
[Nampeyo], and I hope I can keep it up. She was
laughing—I guess she was happy. I know we all
love you. I hope some day we'll be doing like
you're doing so that's why we help you. We all
helped."

*Opposite: Annie Healing Nampeyo
(portrait not available). Pot 3 x 7 ½
in., ca. 1940s. Rick Dillingham collection.*

*Daisy Hooee Nampeyo, ca. 1975
(photographer unknown, courtesy
Daisy Hooee Nampeyo). Pot 2 x 2 ½
in., ca. 1985. Courtesy Buckner/
Lazarus collection, New York.*

Shirley Benn, b. 1936
"I do three things. I make jewelry, I'm a seamstress, and I'm a potter. I like doing pottery sometimes to get away from the jewelry, and I can shape something while watching TV, just to relax. It is something I fall back on when I can't do jewelry. There are times when I get tired of doing jewelry and then I go to pottery. I like to sew also. I sew for my grandkids.

"I learned pottery making from my mom and my grandma, Annie. I lived with her [Annie] during the summers when school was out, and I used to play with her clay."

"My aunt [Rachel Namingha] and my grandma [Annie Healing] used to make pottery for a living. I used to stay in Polacca for the summers. I remember Priscilla [Namingha] made some pots. My mom [Daisy Hooee] was down here [at Zuni], and I wanted to make something for money. My grandma used to tell me to make little pots to sell. I was too small to paint them.

"When I was in Zuni (1955) I really got started in all aspects of pots. I learned jewelry making too. I made jewelry for a living and made pots on the side. A few years ago I started making larger pots."

About Annie: "She used to garden at 'sand hills' during summer. She'd take me and my sister [Luella] up there, and she'd have some clay up there and we'd make little pots. Luella made some turtles not too long ago."

About Nampeyo: "I remember going from Zuni to Polacca to see her [Daisy's] grandmother. I remember her by the door, she was so small and white. She was playing with the dust by the windows. She was blind then."

"I learned most of my pottery from my grandmother, and when I got to doing more my mother helped with shaping. She taught me the ways to make them. The pottery maidens [Zuni Olla Maidens, a performance group that carries large water jars on their heads] would come in summertime, and she [Daisy] would help them make pottery. I learned to mix paint from my mom and learned about the designs, where they come from. I am also a silversmith, I do channel work, necklaces, bolos, and pins."

Opposite: Shirly Benn. Pot 4 x 6 in., ca. 1985. Courtesy Buckner/Lazarus collection, New York.

Top: Juanita Healing (portrait not available). Pot 1 ½ x 6 ½ x 7 ½ in., ca. 1978. Rick Dillingham collection.

Bottom: Cheryl Benn (portrait not available). Pot 4 x 4 in., ca. 1985. Courtesy Buckner/Lazarus collection, New York.

Right: Beatrice Naha Nampeyo (left), ca. 1930. Also pictured: Wesley Lesso (right), Rachel Namingha Nampeyo (center), and Priscilla Namingha Nampeyo (front). Courtesy Daisy Hooee Nampeyo. Pot not available.

Priscilla Namingha Nampeyo, b. 1924
"It's a good thing that I made pots, because it really helps—it helps my children, even my boys. I'm glad God created everything, and without Him we wouldn't be making pots. I always pray when I do my pots, and I tell my children to do the same thing. All of us are getting help from that.

"I learned some from Nampeyo because my grandmother [Annie Healing] didn't do much pottery and my mother [Rachel Namingha] worked with Nampeyo and would help paint and fire for her. Annie was with her [Nampeyo] all the time, and she painted for her too."

Opposite: Rachel Namingha Nampeyo, ca. 1972. Pot 4 1/4 x 8 1/2 in., 1979. Rick Dillingham collection.

Priscilla Namingha Nampeyo. Pot 7 1/2 x 12 in., 1987. Rick Dillingham collection.

Jean Sahme, b. 1949
(Why she leaves the `i' out of Sahmie: "It's simpler for me to spell it that way.")
"I have been happy doing my pottery. It's just gratifying that people enjoy what we do. I don't consider it work—it's something I like to do. We do suffer consequences working on it, but I like it. I share my thoughts in that way, through the pottery.

"What she [Nampeyo] left for us, we still enjoy it. Look how many years it's been since her death [1942], and we still enjoy it. I'm glad I came from an artistic family that can share these things."

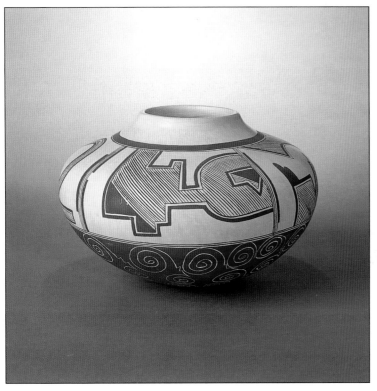

Left: Jean Sahme [note: this spelling is correct]. Pot 6 ½ x 9 ½ in., 1991. Rick Dillingham collection.

Right: Randy Sahmie (portrait not available). Pot 1 ¾ x 5 ¼ x 6 in., 1988. Rick Dillingham inventory.

Opposite: Donella Tom (portrait not available). Pot 1 x 6 in., 1992. Rick Dillingham inventory.

Ida Sahmie, b. 1960
"Personally, I feel I have a unique talent with pottery. It's a combination of both Hopi and Navajo, though I feel it should be more Navajo because I am a Navajo. I want to stick with more Navajo designs. The Yei figures are the most popular for me, secondly would be the rug designs, and third the sand painting designs."

Nyla Sahmie, b. 1954
"I had a great teacher and that's where I owe all my work—and that person is my mother [Priscilla Namingha]."

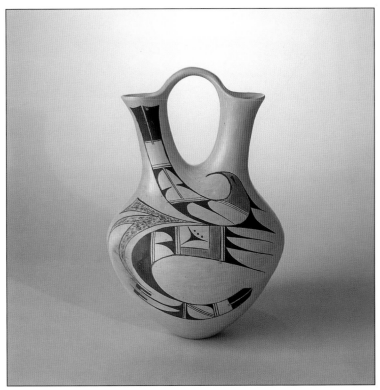

Opposite: Ida Sahmie. Pot 9 x 9 ½ in., 1990. Rick Dillingham collection.

Left: Nyla Sahmie. Pot 14 x 9 in., 1990. Courtesy of the artist.

Right: Michael Collateta (portrait not available). Turtle figure, 1 x 2 ½ in. Rick Dillingham inventory.

Rachel Sahmie, b. 1956
"It [pottery making] is part of my everyday. When you have a child, you make special time. It has automatically fit into everything I do. I don't feel complete if I don't do something on them every-day—even going on a walk for inspiration. It all just fits in, a member of the family."

Bonnie Chapella Nampeyo, b. 1958
"I'm just glad that my mom taught me to make pots, otherwise I don't know where I'd be now. She encouraged me all along. I don't think any-one could be as good a teacher as she."

Opposite: Rachel Sahmie. Pot 5 ½ x 4 in., 1980. Rick Dillingham collection.

Bonnie Chapella Nampeyo. Pot 3 ¼ x 4 in., 1992. Rick Dillingham inventory.

Ruth Namingha James, b. 1926
"First of all, I do some pottery, but all these years I was working for the federal government—twenty-seven years—and I didn't get back into it [pottery]. My other sisters got instruction from my mom, but I was always at work. My children—I had to be home to take care of them on weekends, so I never had time.

"I did do a little [pottery] work when I worked [for the government]. I never did the painting. I helped my mom mold, and she would paint them. I mainly do figurines and pottery with molded animals. I did do some painting on those. They were red clay. I also did some etching [sgraffito]."

Top: Eleanor Lucas (portrait not available). Pot 3 ¾ x 4 ⅝ in., ca. 1988. Courtesy Dewey Galleries, Ltd., Santa Fe.

Bottom: Karen Lucas (portrait not available). Pot 2 x 2 ½ in., 1992. Courtesy Otowi Trading Co., Santa Fe

Opposite: Ruth Namingha James (portrait not available). Storyteller figure, height 5 in., ca. 1985. Courtesy Jim Vigil, Jemez Pueblo.

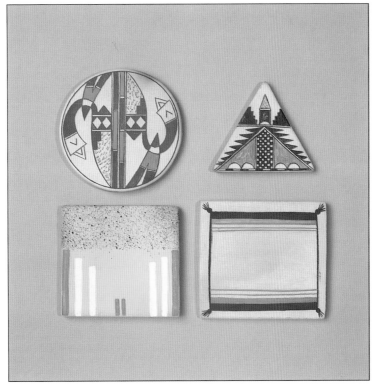

*Darlene Vigil Nampeyo,
b. 1956
"Each pot that I create
gives me a special feel-
ing because I know it is
one of a kind and can
never be duplicated."*

*Top: Stephen Lucas, ca. 1980 (pho-
tographer unknown, courtesy Dextra
Quotskuyva). Opposite: Pot 5 ¼ x 6
in., 1992. Rick Dillingham inventory.*

*Bottom: Darlene Vigil Nampeyo. Four
tiles, 1992: triangle, 3 ½ in.; round,
4 ⅝ in. diameter; "bars," 4 ½ x 4 ½
in.; "manta," 4 ½ x 5 in.. Rick Dillingham collection.*

Les Namingha, b. 1967
(His mother is Zuni)
"Actually, I was looking at some of Dextra's designs and some were old Zuni designs. I want to do more with these designs. The Zuni potters now are using later designs with Spanish motifs. Not many are going back to the old designs from the ruins. I'd like to start doing a lot of these [designs in the Hawikuh book, The Excavation of Hawikuh, by Frederick Webb Hodge; Smith, Woodbury and Woodbury, Reprint, 1966, Musuem of the American Indian, Heye Foundation]. These designs and the designs from around here are an inspiration to me.

"I've been trying to experiment with my own designs, but Dextra says use the old ones first, they have a lot of power, then later add your own ideas. I'd like to incorporate some of the Zuni designs.

"I started four summers ago. My grandmother [Celecita Vicente] at Zuni was inspiring. I picked up something from her in terms of pottery, and four summers ago I really wanted to learn and Dextra offered to help. Dextra is a good teacher. Her work is of high quality, all parts of it. Steve [Lucas], Camille, and I have picked up her standards. We also got a lot of spiritual things from her. It was hard going back and forth to school, and I'd have to begin all over each summer."

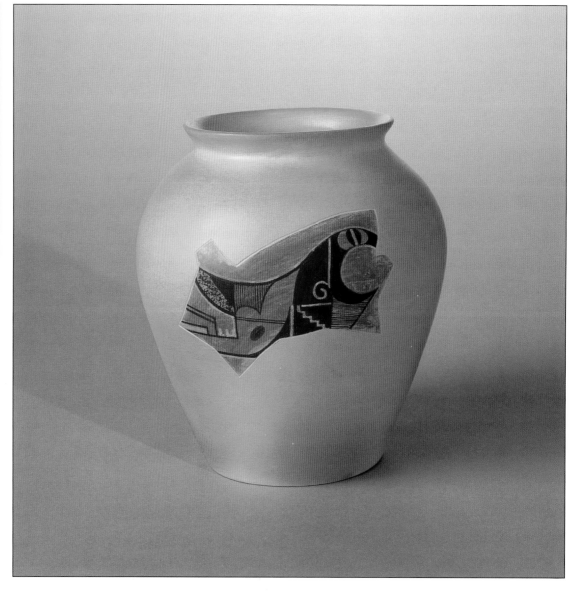

Dextra Quotskuyva Nampeyo, b. 1928
"I think the pottery took over me and I can't get away from it. That's for sure. Clay is in my system. It's all the time, and you're happy with your pots. Camille has been doing real good. I was surprised, I thought she wouldn't continue."

Opposite: Les Namingha. Pot 6 ¾ x 6 ¼ in., 1992. Rick Dillingham inventory.

Dextra Quotskuyva Nampeyo. Pot 3 ¼ x 6 ¾ in., 1978. Rick Dillingham collection.

Camille Hisi Quotskuyva, b. 1964
"I've been doing pots seriously the past four years.
I guess it's always been part of me, since I grew up
with it. I guess it was only natural to do it. It was
hard to learn, and at first I couldn't paint. Mom did
the outlines until I could do it myself. I did sculp-
tural stuff when I couldn't paint. Now I stick to traditional design—now that I can paint."

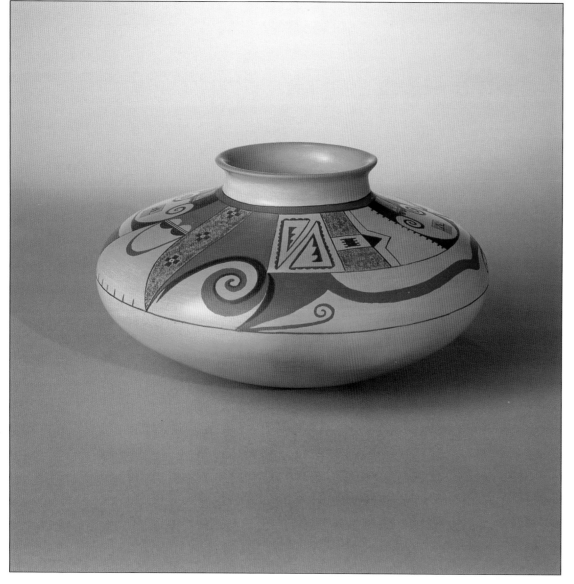

*Top left: Hisi Quotskuyva Nampeyo.
Pot 5 x 9 in., 1992. Rick Dillingham
inventory.*

*Top right: Marie Koopee, ca. 1972.
Pot not available.*

*Bottom right: Nellie Douma Nam-
peyo, ca. 1972. Opposite: Pot 3 ¼ x
7 ½ in., 1979. Rick Dillingham collection.*

The Navasie Family

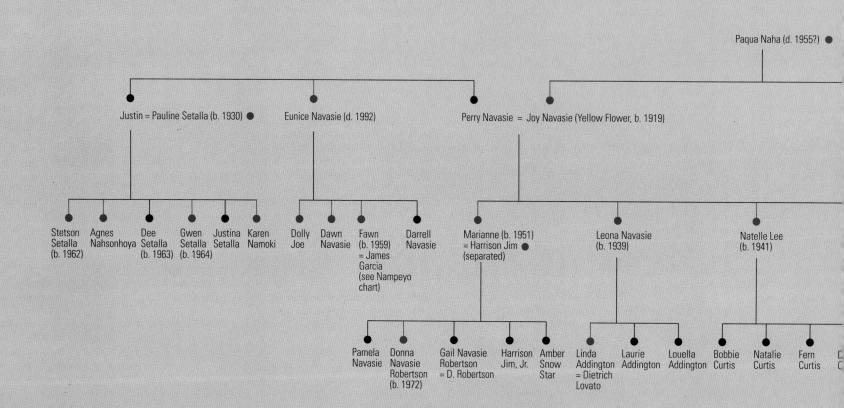

Paqua Naha (d. 1955?) ●

Justin = Pauline Setalla (b. 1930) ●   Eunice Navasie (d. 1992)   Perry Navasie = Joy Navasie (Yellow Flower, b. 1919)

Stetson Setalla (b. 1962)   Agnes Nahsonhoya   Dee Setalla (b. 1963)   Gwen Setalla (b. 1964)   Justina Setalla   Karen Namoki   Dolly Joe   Dawn Navasie   Fawn (b. 1959) = James Garcia (see Nampeyo chart)   Darrell Navasie   Marianne (b. 1951) = Harrison Jim (separated) ●   Leona Navasie (b. 1939)   Natelle Lee (b. 1941)

Pamela Navasie   Donna Navasie Robertson (b. 1972)   Gail Navasie Robertson = D. Robertson   Harrison Jim, Jr.   Amber Snow Star   Linda Addington = Dietrich Lovato   Laurie Addington   Louella Addington   Bobbie Curtis   Natalie Curtis   Fern Curtis

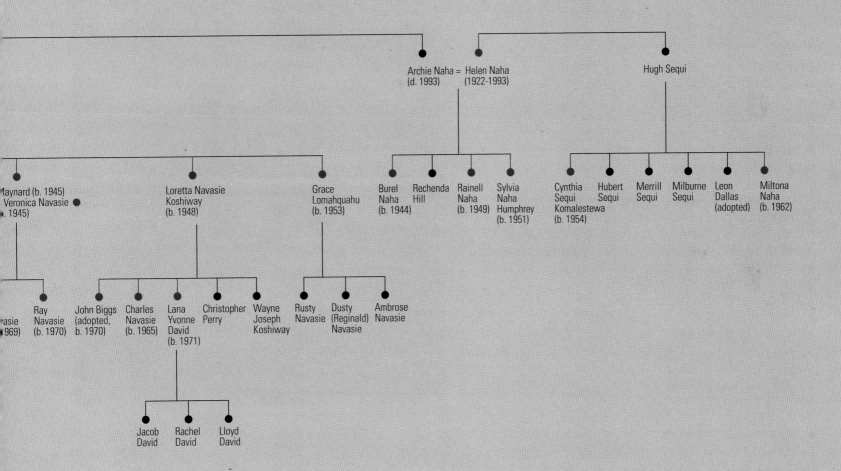

Archie Naha = Helen Naha
(d. 1993)   (1922-1993)

Hugh Sequi

Maynard (b. 1945)
Veronica Navasie
(. 1945)

Loretta Navasie
Koshiway
(b. 1948)

Grace
Lomahquahu
(b. 1953)

Burel
Naha
(b. 1944)

Rechenda
Hill

Rainell
Naha
(b. 1949)

Sylvia
Naha
Humphrey
(b. 1951)

Cynthia
Sequi
Komalestewa
(b. 1954)

Hubert
Sequi

Merrill
Sequi

Milburne
Sequi

Leon
Dallas
(adopted)

Miltona
Naha
(b. 1962)

vasie
969)

Ray
Navasie
(b. 1970)

John Biggs
(adopted,
b. 1970)

Charles
Navasie
(b. 1965)

Lana
Yvonne
David
(b. 1971)

Christopher
Perry

Wayne
Joseph
Koshiway

Rusty
Navasie

Dusty
(Reginald)
Navasie

Ambrose
Navasie

Jacob
David

Rachel
David

Lloyd
David

61

Joy Navasie, b. 1919 ("But I have three birthdays, 1916 and 1918 also!")
She signs her pottery solely with the Frog symbol. "Every day we wake up to the same thing. It's a job we rely on, it's our livelihood. It's within us so much it just comes everyday. It's the only thing I'm really happy with. I enjoy my work. For a while I had to leave it when I got sick, and then the doctor said I could return to work.

"I've grown into the white slip [characteristic of the family's pottery] when my mother [Paqua] was alive. She did a beige and yellow pottery and started the white slip not long—three to four years—before she passed away. She didn't do much red. I did some little ones I remember in yellow clay. I used to put a flower drawing under my pot 'Yellow Flower' is my Indian name then I began to use my mother's trademark.

"When I was about twenty I started using the Frog. I made pottery before I married, I was a teenager—sixteen or seventeen. I feel good the slipped pottery has become recognized. It's hard to polish the slip. Everything is traditional—gathering the clay, the molding, coiling the pots, slipping, polishing, and painting them, and firing with sheep dung. The sheep manure is getting hard to get, but we haven't gotten into commercial stuff and I hope these girls don't do that. I want them to respect the Frog, my mother's work. I have pride in her Frog."

Joy Navasie. Pot 10 x 7 ½ in., 1981. Rick Dillingham collection.

Paqua Naha, ca. 1945? (photographer unknown, courtesy Maynard and Veronica Navasie). Opposite: Pot 8 ½ x 11 in., ca. 1950. Rick Dillingham collection.

Loretta Navasie Koshiway, b. 1948
She formerly signed her pottery with a Frog and the initial L.; now many carry just the Frog symbol. Joy Navasie does the painting.
"I still work closely with my mom. She outlines her own and I help her fill in and I'll help her mold. It's a process we go through, we'll pass them back and forth. I owe everything to her. She's taught me everything and without her we wouldn't have come this far. She taught us to thank the Mother Earth. All our work comes from nature."

Charles Navasie, b. 1965
"I owe it all to my grandmother [Joy Navasie]. She's the one who taught me. I kept working at it and I see an improvement in my work. The past three years she did my designing, and now I'm doing it. I'm trying to improve myself even further. My designs are similar to hers. I can never repay all my grandmother's help, and now I can help her. Putting back a little to help her out."

John Biggs, b. 1970
"I did some [pottery] in high school, it was a Native American art class. I learned to coil pottery and I came out here [Hopi] and kept on going. I was always drawing, since grade school and then I went to take art classes in Lawrence, Kansas. I started making pottery here with my mom and grandma. They inspired me and told me to keep up the good work and go to school."

Opposite left: Charles Navasie. Pot not available.

Opposite right: Loretta Navasie Koshiway. Pot 5 x 6 in., ca. 1988. Courtesy Buckner/Lazarus collection, New York.

John Biggs (portrait not available). Pot 2 ½ x 3 ¼ in., 1992. Rick Dillingham inventory.

Leona Navasie, b. 1939
Her pottery in the recent past was signed with the Frog symbol and the initials L.N.
"I think the reason I took interest in it—out of the family, my sisters anyway—I knew my grandmother [Paqua Naha], and I stayed with her and saw the work she did. It was a necessity at the time and wasn't appreciated as art. My mom's [Joy Navasie] gotten to be pretty well known, and she talks to me of the source of naturalness of the ingredients, the significance of everything, [from] collecting clay to the preparation of the paints.

"I was raised off the reservation in the belagana world. I can see now looking back I didn't appreciate my grandmother enough when she was alive. When I came back home, when my mom was in her heyday—the eighties—lots of shows, traveling, magazines—and that's when I got into potting with her. I use it almost like therapy when I get a little depressed."

Grace Lomahquahu,
b. 1953
Her pottery has been
signed with the Frog
symbol and the initial G.
*"To tell the honest truth,
I've never had anything
to do with the yellow pottery. Doing the white
pots I learned from my
mother. The yellow would
come hard for me and
the white hard for them
[potters in the yellow
style], an exchange. I'm
always glad someone
wants to buy pottery.
You create it and it
feeds you. It's keeping
us alive and going.*

*"I guess mainly my
designs are similar to
hers [Joy Navasie]—
traditional. I try to keep
it similar to hers rather
than modernize it or
make it fancy."*

*Opposite: Leona Navasie. Pot 5 x 4
in., ca. 1987. Courtesy Buckner/
Lazarus collection, New York.*

*Grace Lomahquahu. Pot 6 x 7 in.,
1992. Rick Dillingham inventory.*

Maynard Navasie, b. 1945, and Veronica Navasie, b. 1945
They sign their pottery with a Frog and their initials.
Maynard: *"My mother-in-law [Laura Preston from Walpi] taught my wife, and I was really started by my mom [Joy Navasie] but the designing was my own. Ronnie [Veronica] has always done the molding, and I sand, polish, and paint. Pottery to our family is everything. It has paid for all our food and has helped in every way. It has also gotten us to know a lot of people who enjoy our work. I do the red slip when someone asks for it, but we usually do white-slipped pots. We use the Frog to carry the Navasie name."*

Bill Navasie, b.1969
He signs his pottery with a Frog, musical notes, and his initials.
"I just meet a lot of new people from the U.S., Japan, and Germany—people who travel a long way to look at Hopi art."

*Maynard and Veronica Navasie.
Pots: tile, 6 ¼ in. tall, ca. 1982, Rick Dillingham collection; opposite: 7 x 6 in., 1990, Rick Dillingham inventory.*

Marianne Navasie Jim, b. 1951
Her pottery in the recent past was signed with a Frog symbol and a tadpole drawing.
"As for me, I really enjoy my work. I used to sit here and watch my mom [Joy Navasie]. I wanted to learn the art of painting my own pottery, and it took a few years to learn [Joy would paint]. It relaxes my mind when I do it, although it can be tiring. I admire where it came from, from Paqua to my mom. I started when I was about twenty-five years old and my mother used to design them and we would sign them with a pollywog and M.N. [in addition to the family's Frog motif].

"There's too much contemporary [commercial and/or kiln-fired] pottery that we find hard to compete with. Even my girls have gotten into this contemporary work. We decided we needed to label them that way. My mother wants us to stick to traditional, stick to the old way."

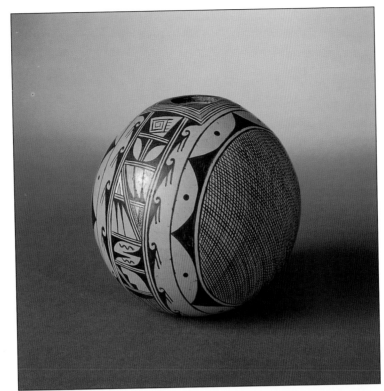

Donna Robertson,
b. 1972
"I got started when I was going to school. When I wanted something, my mom said, 'Go to work,' so I started making pottery—to work for what I want. I haven't tried anything else but the white style. It's the way I was taught. I haven't tried much out of the tradition, though I have done some small frog sculptures."

Cynthia Sequi, b. 1954
"I've been doing this for about six years. I kind of played around with clay when my maternal grandmother did it and I came down and worked with Sylvia [Naha], and then I started on my own. I would help her paint and then tried my own. I'm more Hopi than I am Tewa, so my pots are more Hopi style. Mine are a natural color and she [Sylvia] uses a white slip. I stayed with the brushes [commercial paintbrushes] after learning how to fill in with them."

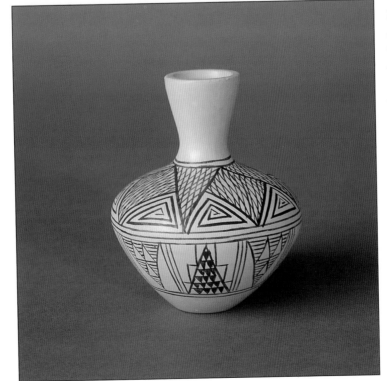

Opposite: Marianne Navasie. Pot 9 x 6 in., 1992. Rick Dillingham inventory.

Top: Cynthia Sequi Komalestewa. Pot 3 ½ x 3 ½ in., 1992. Courtesy Andrews Pueblo Pottery, Albuquerque.

Bottom: Miltona Naha (portrait not available). Pot 3 x 2 ½ in., 1992. Rick Dillingham inventory.

Helen Naha (Feather Woman), b. 1922, d. 1993
"I started around 1945–46 because of financial problems we had after the war to support my family. It was hard for me to do it without a teacher. I had to teach myself. It took me a longer time to get used to it. The designs came from Awatovi ruins. Archie [her husband] and I used to put different designs together and came up with original combinations. He helped me with the clay, but I had to do the work all by myself. It took me six years for my pottery to start selling.

"I made a lot of mistakes because I taught myself. I like the black and white designs the best. I used to paint my pottery like Joy Navasie, and then I got my own designs from the sherds [at Awatovi ruin]. I watched Archie's mom, Paqua. I use a few designs with many variations."

Helen Naha. Pot 5 ½ x 11 ½ in., ca. 1979. Rick Dillingham collection.

Opposite: Burel Naha. Pot 5 ½ x 8 ½ in., 1992. Rick Dillingham inventory.

Burel Naha, b. 1944
"As far as getting start-
ed, I owe it to my moth-
er [Helen Naha]. I got
started late because I
had a teaching position.
I used to work in the
summer when school
was out.

"The designs I was using
earlier were my mom's,
and a year and a half
ago my daughter Cindy
came home with a pic-
ture of a spider. She said
they were doing [draw-
ing] them at school.
About two or three weeks
later, at 3 a.m. with that
on my mind, I couldn't
find the drawing. When
I found it, I started using
spider designs on my
pots. A lot of people call
me Spider Man, and
I've gone off with my
own designs.

"It's refreshing to work
with my hands. Being
an art teacher got me
going."

Sylvia Naha, b. 1951
She signs her pottery with a Feather and the initial S.
"A lot of my designs are in part some of Mom's [Helen Naha] designs, and I just mix them. There are about five designs of hers I use in different ways. Sometimes I used to cover up crooked designs and fit others to it.

"I'm starting to mix my designs with more traditional designs. A lot of people like the animal designs and a lot like the traditional, so I mix them. People like to see a lot of fineline, and others like the simplicity. I like to bounce back and forth, to make something eye pleasing. I don't understand what the design meant before so I use them to make something someone will like."

Rainell (Rainy) Naha, b. 1949
"I've been around pots most all my life growing up. I didn't see it as I do today. A young person sees things differently. It was a burden to make finances come together, so we helped our mom [Helen Naha]. It was a chore, but at that time I really didn't understand it. I left at eight and moved to Utah, and I'd come home every summer. I didn't have too much social interaction with the villagers.

"I came back in 1989. I wanted to find my roots. I needed to come home, and I wanted to learn this [pottery making] while I had the greatest teacher alive [Helen Naha]. There's been a tremendous amount of growth, and I see myself as an artist in traditional pots. I know what I need to stay within those limits. I'm a potter, a competitive runner, I raise cattle, and I volunteer at the high school. I tried my hand at politics, and that only lasted a year!"

Sylvia Naha Humphrey. Opposite: Pot 5 ½ x 5 in., 1992. Courtesy Andrews Pueblo Pottery, Albuquerque.

Rainelle Naha. Pot 4 ½ x 4 ¼ in., 1992. Rick Dillingham inventory.

Opposite: Dawn Navasie. Pot 5 x 8 in., 1992. Courtesy McGees Indian Art, Keams Canyon, Arizona.

Fawn Garcia, b. 1959
"I used to do the white pottery with my mom [Eunice Navasie], and now I do the yellow style with James. It's hard to get the white. I like doing the white—it's harder. I still like to carry on my mother's designs, since I learned from her. I try to experiment with different types of designs. I do most of the molding, I polish, then we do the painting together. I think we're doing good and there's a lot of improvement in our work. We'll get better at it!"

Pauline Setalla, b. 1930
"I learned from my mother-in-law, Agnes Navasie, my husband's mother, around 1954. His name is Justin. I do white pottery, but I got tired of white-washing, so now I'm doing some natural yellow and red clay. I taught all my children. I'm from Second Mesa and married here. I use mostly corn designs, yellow clouds, snow, and stairways. I also use pueblo houses [drawings of them] and lightning."

Dee Johnson Setalla, b. 1963
"I've been making since I was small. I learned everything from my mom. I quit when I went to school, and when I finished I started up again. Since I'm not working at a job I do pottery fulltime."

Opposite: Fawn Navasie Garcia. Pot 7 x 6 ¼ in., ca. 1988. Courtesy Dewey Galleries, Ltd., Santa Fe.

Top: Pauline Setalla. Pot not available.

Bottom: Dee Setalla. Pot not available.

Stetson Setalla (portrait not available). Pot 3 ½ x 9 ¾ in., 1992. Courtesy McGees Indian Art, Keams Canyon, Arizona.

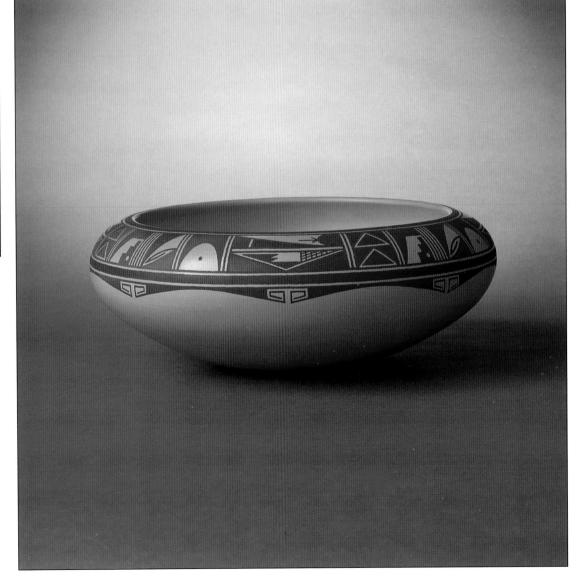

Acoma Pueblo

The Chino Family

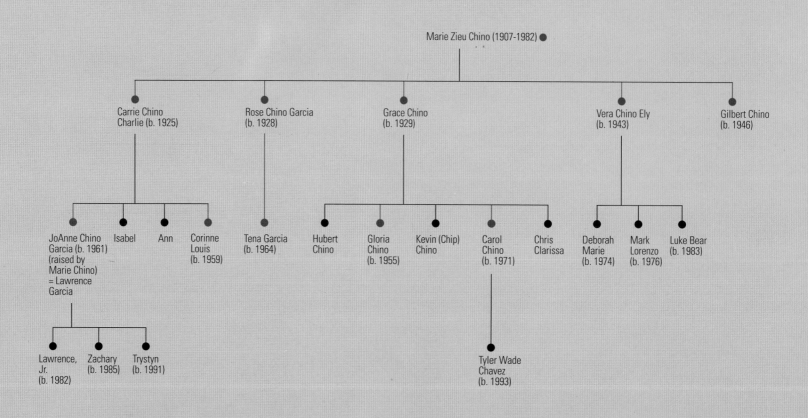

Marie Zieu Chino (1907-1982)

Carrie Chino Charlie (b. 1925)

Rose Chino Garcia (b. 1928)

Grace Chino (b. 1929)

Vera Chino Ely (b. 1943)

Gilbert Chino (b. 1946)

JoAnne Chino Garcia (b. 1961) (raised by Marie Chino) = Lawrence Garcia

Isabel

Ann

Corinne Louis (b. 1959)

Tena Garcia (b. 1964)

Hubert Chino

Gloria Chino (b. 1955)

Kevin (Chip) Chino

Carol Chino (b. 1971)

Chris Clarissa

Deborah Marie (b. 1974)

Mark Lorenzo (b. 1976)

Luke Bear (b. 1983)

Lawrence, Jr. (b. 1982)

Zachary (b. 1985)

Trystyn (b. 1991)

Tyler Wade Chavez (b. 1993)

Tena Garcia, b. 1964
"I do miniatures. I like doing the Mimbres designs, and I do smaller pieces, and I help Rose [Chino Garcia] out on her bigger pieces. Rose taught me how to make pottery. I like making small seed pots and small versions of old jars. I want to learn how to make big pots in the future."

Previous page: Marie Zieu Chino. Pot 13 x 8 ½ in., 1979. Rick Dillingham collection.

Marie Zieu Chino, ca. 1972. Pot 9 x 11 ½ in., 1981. Rick Dillingham collection.

Tena Garcia. Pot not available.

Opposite: Rose Chino Garcia. Pot 7 x 8 in., 1992. Rick Dillingham inventory.

Rose Chino Garcia, b. 1928
"I enjoy doing it. I learned it from my mom [Marie Z. Chino] and just kept it up. She's no longer here. It's been doing real good for me and my daughter [Tena]. I'm trying to stick to Marie's designs. I always did the tall-necked shapes. I also do plates with potsherd designs. I've invented some designs myself. I want to continue doing pots and add on new designs and shapes when I can."

Carrie Chino Charlie, b. 1925
"I said, 'Mom [Marie Z. Chino], show me how to make pottery,' and then she started teaching me. I was very interested in making, but I didn't learn it right away. I started helping her fill in her painting, then she started teaching me all of it. She started taking me to the markets, and then I began to teach my children. I learned the fineline design from my mom and have continued to use it. My daughters Isabel and Ann help me paint it now."

JoAnn Chino Garcia (portrait not available). Pot 4 ¼ x 4 ½ in., 1989. Rick Dillingham collection.

Opposite: Carrie Chino Charlie. Pot 8 ¼ x 11 ¼ in., ca. 1985. Rick Dillingham collection.

Gilbert Chino, b. 1946
"I value traditional pottery very much. It's a shame that some people have to mix commercial clay with real clay. From there it makes it difficult for those who use traditional stuff. During Indian Market it's like going to a flea market, because they really don't judge on traditional pottery. There's no way the colors you see are natural—we don't have those colors. We don't get as much as our work is worth when tourists don't know the difference between commercial and traditional. I do tell them what the difference is at the house when they come to buy. I want to be able to get what I put into it."

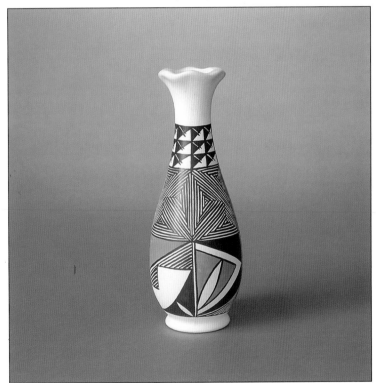

Opposite: Gilbert Chino. Pot with commercial black paint, 6 x 6 ½ in., 1989. Rick Dillingham collection.

Corrine Louis (portrait not available). Commercial ceramic pot, 7 x 2 ¾ in., ca. 1989. Courtesy Carrie Charlie.

Grace Chino, b. 1929

"When I first started it seemed easy, and now when I learned more it has become more enjoyable. I enjoy working. I like to work alone, with both the potting and painting. When I'm doing my pottery I think of mom [Marie Z. Chino] first, and that she could help me. I want to do like she does. She didn't need outlining, she just painted, and sometimes I do that now. I know the design and I just do it."

Grace Chino. Pot 8 ½ x 9 in., 1991, painted by Gloria Chino. Rick Dillingham inventory.

Top right: Gloria Chino (pot not available).

Bottom right: Vera Chino Ely (portrait courtesy Mark Ely). Opposite: Pot 7 x 8 ¼ in., ca. 1979, made by Marie Z. Chino and painted by Vera Chino Ely.

The Lewis Family

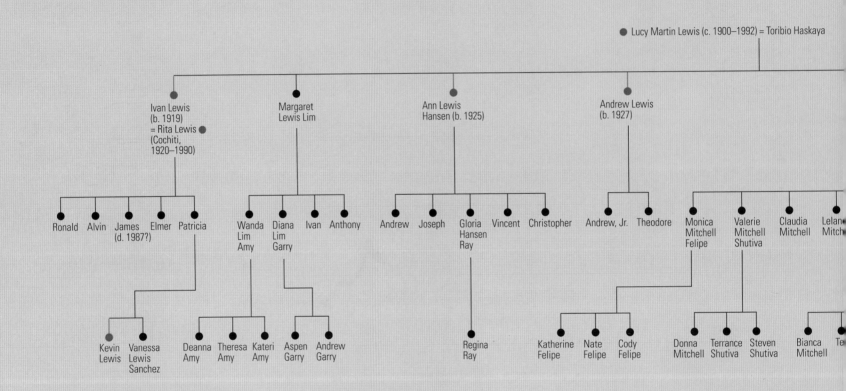

● Lucy Martin Lewis (c. 1900–1992) = Toribio Haskaya

Ivan Lewis
(b. 1919)
= Rita Lewis ●
(Cochiti,
1920–1990)

Margaret
Lewis Lim

Ann Lewis
Hansen (b. 1925)

Andrew Lewis
(b. 1927)

Ronald   Alvin   James   Elmer   Patricia
                 (d. 1987?)

Wanda   Diana   Ivan   Anthony
Lim   Lim
Amy   Garry

Andrew   Joseph   Gloria   Vincent   Christopher
                  Hansen
                  Ray

Andrew, Jr.   Theodore

Monica   Valerie   Claudia   Lelan
Mitchell   Mitchell   Mitchell   Mitch
Felipe   Shutiva

Kevin   Vanessa
Lewis   Lewis
         Sanchez

Deanna   Theresa   Kateri
Amy   Amy   Amy

Aspen   Andrew
Garry   Garry

Regina
Ray

Katherine   Nate   Cody
Felipe   Felipe   Felipe

Donna   Terrance   Steven
Mitchell   Shutiva   Shutiva

Bianca   Te
Mitchell

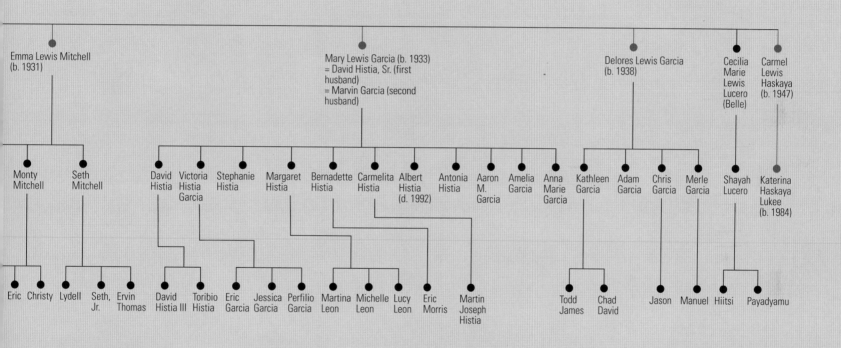

Emma Lewis Mitchell
(b. 1931)

Mary Lewis Garcia (b. 1933)
= David Histia, Sr. (first
husband)
= Marvin Garcia (second
husband)

Delores Lewis Garcia
(b. 1938)

Cecilia
Marie
Lewis
Lucero
(Belle)

Carmel
Lewis
Haskaya
(b. 1947)

Monty
Mitchell

Seth
Mitchell

David
Histia

Victoria
Histia
Garcia

Stephanie
Histia

Margaret
Histia

Bernadette
Histia

Carmelita
Histia

Albert
Histia
(d. 1992)

Antonia
Histia

Aaron
M.
Garcia

Amelia
Garcia

Anna
Marie
Garcia

Kathleen
Garcia

Adam
Garcia

Chris
Garcia

Merle
Garcia

Shayah
Lucero

Katerina
Haskaya
Lukee
(b. 1984)

Eric   Christy   Lydell   Seth,   Ervin
                            Jr.   Thomas

David   Toribio
Histia III   Histia

Eric   Jessica   Perfilio
Garcia   Garcia   Garcia

Martina   Michelle   Lucy
Leon   Leon   Leon

Eric
Morris

Martin
Joseph
Histia

Todd   Chad
James   David

Jason   Manuel   Hiitsi   Payadyamu

Lucy Martin Lewis, 1980. Pots: 5 x 9 in., 1991, Rick Dillingham inventory; opposite: 5 x 6 ¼ in., ca. 1965, Rick Dillingham collection.

Ivan Lewis, b. 1919
"I never made Acoma pottery. When Rita's mother was getting older, she [Rita] took an interest in pottery. Her mother was a good potter and taught pottery making at the Indian schools in Santa Fe and Albuquerque. Rita learned from her mother, like my mother [Lucy M. Lewis] passed it to our family. We were married in 1944, and I moved to Cochiti. I was in the service and was discharged in 1946 or so. I decided to make my home here [at Cochiti]. Rita started [making pottery] around 1959. The dam [Cochiti Lake dam] started around 1965, and I worked on it for twelve years. I started pottery with her [Rita] around 1977. We used to work with silver, too. I didn't learn pottery from my mom, I learned from Rita. I started making different figures: cowboys, mermaids. I make them in the traditional way. I'm having a hard time getting the slip [white base slip], so sometimes I have to use some commercial paint when I don't have enough.

"You [Rick] got me started on mermaids with an order you gave me. People ask how I got started, and I tell them I used to talk to the mermaids at Cochiti Lake. They would come out around midnight. I'm the only one who knows where they are."

Lucy Martin Lewis, 1980. Two pieces: turkey figure, 4 in. high, 1991, and bird figure, 3 ½ in. long, 1991, both Rick Dillingham inventory.

Opposite: Ivan Lewis. Mermaid figure by Ivan and Rita Lewis, ca. 1987, 6 ½ x 10 ½ in.. Rick Dillingham collection.

Anne Lewis Hansen, b. 1925

"In 1935 or so, my brother and I used to sell the pottery with Mom [Lucy M. Lewis] along Route 66, before I went away to boarding school. I used to help Mom grind the sherds for clay. I started miniatures when she got the clay ready. In the 1950s I began to go to Indian Market and Gallup. Eventually, I got my own booth [after sharing with her mother].

"I left in 1944 and went to California, and I've lived there since. I come home every year. Now that Lucy is gone [d. 1991], I won't make it [home] as much. I like making pottery. I graduated from San Jose State with a history major. There's no problem working in California doing traditional Acoma pottery. I've helped jury shows in California, and I give classes and presentations on pottery."

Andrew Lewis, b. 1927
"When I first started, I figured it was only for women but I decided one day I wanted to make pottery. I asked my mom [Lucy Lewis] for some clay. She said, 'When it's gone, you know where it is to get your own.'

"As far as I know—or the stories I've heard—there was a man-woman [potter]. My late father knew him. I had an urge to make pottery, but my father didn't make. I use the Mimbres [designs], and mostly I stay with Acoma traditional designs. I'm trying to out-do some of the potters who do big pots. To date I've made one 22 inches in height and about 32 inches in diameter. I'm going to make bigger ones still."

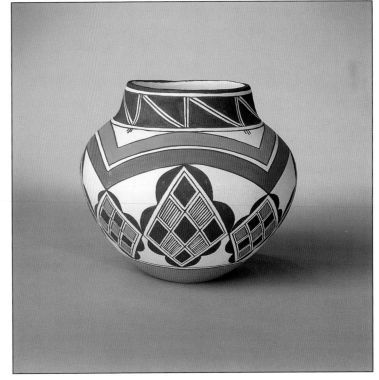

Opposite: Anne Lewis Hansen. Pot 4 x 5 in., ca. 1982. Courtesy Delores Lewis Garcia.

Left: Kevin Lewis (Morningstar) (portrait not available). Animal figure 6 ½ x 9 in., 1992. Courtesy Buckner/ Lazarus collection, New York.

Right: Andrew Lewis. Pot 5 ½ x 6 ½ in., 1992. Rick Dillingham inventory.

Emma Lewis Mitchell, b. 1931
"I started about the 1960s. I found an old pot dated 1972 the other day. I'm sticking with the Mimbres designs. I want to keep them alive by continuing to use them—try to keep them as the Mimbres people painted them. I feel a spiritual connection to them. I think we're all connected some way. The archae-ologists say, Where did the ancient people go? What about us? We're the new generation.

"There's a lot of good things to say about my moth-er. She was my inspiration, and without her encouragement, her help and guidance, I wouldn't be where I am today."

Mary Lewis Garcia, b. 1933
"I'm strictly sticking to traditional polychrome designs. Once in a while I'll do others—Chaco, Mesa Verde, or Mimbres—but I prefer to do Acoma Polychrome. I like to do the traditional olla form, miniatures, and large, and I like to make serving bowls and canteens. I also like to do Mesa Verde mugs and ladles and corrugated cooking pots.

"About commercial pottery: I wish they would go back to the traditional way of pottery making. It has more meaning. The materials are all there for us from the earth."

Opposite: Emma Lewis Mitchell. Pot 7 x 7 in., 1992. Rick Dillingham inventory.

Delores Lewis Garcia, b. 1938
"My greatest inspiration is from the ancient people, the Anasazi. If it weren't for them, we wouldn't be doing the pots. The best of all inspiration is my mom, Lucy. If it weren't for her, I wouldn't be making any pots. I think it's good we talk about our pottery [the family does a lot of public demonstration] because not everyone knows about Indian pottery. I think the non-Indian should hear it from a potter. From there, I think they understand the true feeling of Indian art, where the designs come from and where we came from—the Ancient People. Generation to generation, we keep the pottery rolling."

Opposite: Delores Lewis Garcia. Pot 3 x 5 in., 1991. Rick Dillingham inventory.

Carmel Lewis Haskaya with her daughter Katerina Haskaya Lukee. Pots: Left: Katerina Haskaya Lukee. 1 ½ x 1 ¾ in. (painted by Carmel). Right: Carmel Lewis Haskaya. Pot 4 x 6 in., 1991. Both Rick Dillingham inventory.

ZIA PUEBLO

The Medina Family

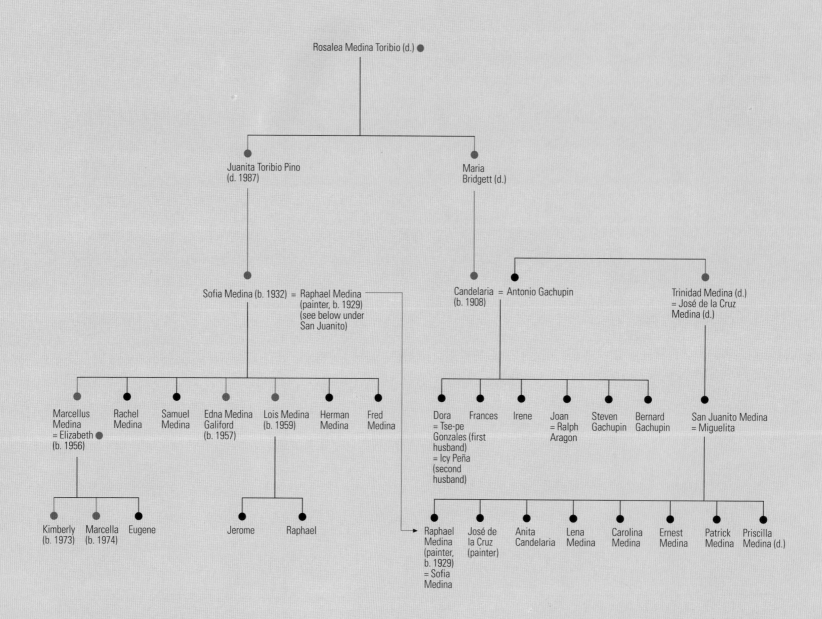

Rosalea Medina Toribio (d.)

Juanita Toribio Pino (d. 1987)

Maria Bridgett (d.)

Sofia Medina (b. 1932) = Raphael Medina (painter, b. 1929) (see below under San Juanito)

Candelaria (b. 1908) = Antonio Gachupin

Trinidad Medina (d.) = José de la Cruz Medina (d.)

Marcellus Medina = Elizabeth (b. 1956)

Rachel Medina

Samuel Medina

Edna Medina Galiford (b. 1957)

Lois Medina (b. 1959)

Herman Medina

Fred Medina

Dora = Tse-pe Gonzales (first husband) = Icy Peña (second husband)

Frances

Irene

Joan = Ralph Aragon

Steven Gachupin

Bernard Gachupin

San Juanito Medina = Miguelita

Kimberly (b. 1973)

Marcella (b. 1974)

Eugene

Jerome

Raphael

Raphael Medina (painter, b. 1929) = Sofia Medina

José de la Cruz (painter)

Anita Candelaria

Lena Medina

Carolina Medina

Ernest Medina

Patrick Medina

Priscilla Medina (d.)

Trinidad Medina, ca. 1925?, with Priscilla (deceased), Patrick, Ernest, Rose (deceased), Carolina and Trinidad (deceased). (Courtesy Sofia Medina, Zia.) Pot approximately 18 x 20 in., ca. 1925. Collection of Frank Sorauf, Minneapolis.

Opposite: J.D. (José de la Cruz) Medina (portrait not available). Pot made by Sofia Medina with acrylic painting by J. D. Medina, 8 x 10 ½ in., ca. 1975. Courtesy Margaret Gutierrez, Santa Clara Pueblo.

Top: Juanita Pino (portrait not available). Pot 10 ¼ x 11 in., 1950. Courtesy Museum of Indian Art and Culture/ Laboratory of Anthropology, Santa Fe.

Bottom: Sofia Medina. Pot 9 ½ x 11 in., 1992. Rick Dillingham inventory.

Sofia Medina, b. 1932

"I got into making potteries in 1963 after returning from California—I lived there a while. Raphael's [her husband] grandmother, Trinidad, started to show me how to make them. I started enjoying it. It made me feel that instead of sitting around, it was something I loved to do. I didn't do it for money. It was very consoling if I was depressed, and when I got back to pots it gave me a lot of relief. I talked to them. It's something that I hold in my heart. When I'm not doing my pottery, I'm not happy.

"In maybe 1954 I encouraged him [Raphael] to paint, and he did [acrylic] painting on paper. It was the same thing with him—he enjoyed painting, something he loved to do. I think he started painting on my pots in the seventies. He used natural pigments on only two of them."

"Spiritually, the pottery can ease your mind. I do sing a lot when I am working . . . worse than a radio!"

About Trinidad Medina: "She always told me instead of sitting around after the children went to school to work on pottery. Pottery making was important. Financially she could depend on that. She said she'd teach me—but first, tell me and promise me whatever I teach you, pass it on to my grandchildren so in the future they will profit from it and in the future my work would continue."

Sofia to her grandchildren: "I've talked to them and explained to them, pottery is a hard job. And I told them, I don't know how long this pottery business will be good, so get an education. In case you are laid off a job, you will have something to fall back on, a financial backup."

Opposite: Sofia Medina. Pot by Sofia Medina and acrylic painting done by Raphael, 1979, SAR 1979-10, courtesy Indian Art Research Center, School of American Research.

Lois Medina, b. 1959

"I try to make my pottery distinctive in shape, form, and design, and I'm trying to do different styles and designs. I do a lot of research on my own, designs from other pueblos, and I mix them with mine. Then I go back to the old pottery and learn the meaning of each design.

"When I started working, my grandma [Sofia's mother, Juanita Pino] sat me down and told me the story behind pottery, how it was created—the true meaning behind it. She gave me everything—some old purse with old tools, gourds, brushes, black stone [for painting]—I won't use it, it's too precious. I had others made."

About Trinidad: "Trinidad had a lot of impact on me, though I didn't know her on a personal level well. Her design was so unique. I knew her as an old woman. I never really got to talk to her."

Rachel Medina, b. 1961
"Well, I went to school for a while, vocational school for a nursing degree, and I went to Eastern in Portales for a while. When I had my kids, I decided to do pots more seriously. Now I'm picking it up again.

"I stay down at old Santa Ana, where my fiancé is from, and I joked about reviving pottery there! I do the traditional style like my mom, but she tells me my designs are leaning to Santa Ana style, with more flowers and stuff. My mom told me they look Santa Ana. There's a lady teaching me the different Santa Ana designs, Eudora Montoya.

"With all the inspiration and guidance and support the family gives to one another, it's good to have them. It makes you feel you can do whatever you want in the art, and you feel successful."

Edna Galiford, b. 1957
"My work is very contemporary—I'm not traditional, I guess you could call it.
I try to keep a little tradition and keep with my father's style. I use a lot of contemporary bold designs, but the figures are traditional. I do painting on matte boards with bold colors, and the paintings I do on wood are more natural colors.

"On the pots, I do an in-between style. It's not very traditional—I mix everything up on the pots. I guess I'm trying to create my own style. I'm trying to make my own name—independence. I can't get away from the Medina name, everyone knows it.

"I have a degree in art education and commercial art. I taught two years at the Christian School and the public school in Gallup. Then I quit and started doing my art. I taught in Portales one year, too. I come home on special occasions—feast and Christmas."

Opposite: Lois Medina. Pot 10 1/2 x 7 3/4 in., 1993. Rick Dillingham inventory.

Left: Rachel Medina. Pot not available.

Right: Edna Medina Galiford. Pot not available.

Marcellus Medina, b. 1954

"Me and Liz work with acrylic-painted pottery. She makes the pottery and fires it. After that stage, I take it, sand it, and work on it with acrylic paint. The natural [native pigment] ones I do are small—three to four inches—and I make the small ones. I don't produce them in huge quantity. I don't work on very large pieces.

"It was 1976 when I started. My father was teaching me, getting me used to painting figures on the pot itself. It's really hard. At the beginning I traced a figure of a dancer on a flat surface and then traced it on the pot, but the figure wasn't the same. It was all broken up—it didn't look right. It looked more like Picasso's figures! Instead of tracing, I sketch on the pot itself.

"My mom is really traditional. She really believes in traditional ways. For me and Liz it's half and half, part traditional and part contemporary. For an Indian artist to succeed they have to change with the times, and we have to appeal to Anglo art tastes. It's really difficult for my parents to understand, and we still debate it—old and new generations. We still believe in tradition but also in the new age."

Opposite: Elizabeth Medina. Pot 10 ½ x 11 in., 1992. Courtesy of the artist. Rachel Medina. Pot not available.

Marcellus Medina. Pot made by Elizabeth Medina and painted in acrylic by Marcellus Medina, 3 ¾ x 3 ½ in., 1990. Courtesy Buckner/ Lazarus collection, New York.

Elizabeth Medina, b. 1956
"I used to make pottery when I was a child, but they were Jemez pottery [Liz was born at Jemez]. I started making Zia pots after I was married in 1978 and got tribal permission. My mother-in-law, Sofia, is my inspiration. She always gets the credit, and I make sure she does!

"I still make the larger pots for Marcellus to paint. I had to learn a lot, because it's different from the Jemez pottery—the clay is different and so are the paints.

"The black rock is what we use for temper. Basalt. We pound it into chunks, then to powder. It's difficult to do. We bury chunks of rock by the river and let freezing help deteriorate it. Once it's dug up, it's a little easier to prepare. It's Mother Nature helping with erosion. We leave them for two or three years.

"With our business, we're looking at a lot of changes, and we want to make more and change the style to something different where we can interest the public."

Elizabeth Medina.

Opposite left: Kimberly Medina. Top: Pot 5 ¾ x 7 in., 1993. Courtesy of the artist.

Opposite right: Marcella Medina. Bottom: Pot 5 ½ x 6 ½ in., 1993. Courtesy of the artist.

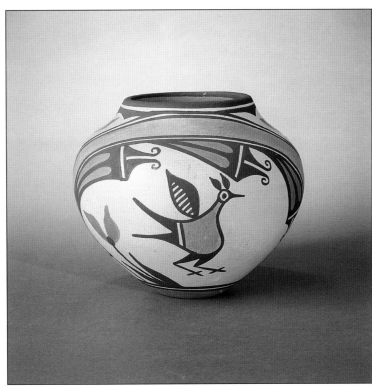

Kimberly Medina,
b. 1973
"It's very interesting to learn about my family's history and where tradition came from—and that my family is still carrying on these traditions, passed from generation to generation. At first, when I started, it was exciting to do something different. Now that I'm older and going to school, I want to find out what's out there for me. I make during the summer when I'm not in school and when I need to make some extra money.

"It's hard for me to decide which direction to go. School is the most important thing for me now."

Marcella Medina,
b. 1974
"I only make small ones for spending money. Right now I'm not totally into pots, I'm still in high school. I do little traditional pots and sometimes I paint them. I wanted to do acrylic-painted pots, but it's hard. I don't have the patience."

COCHITI

The Herrera Family

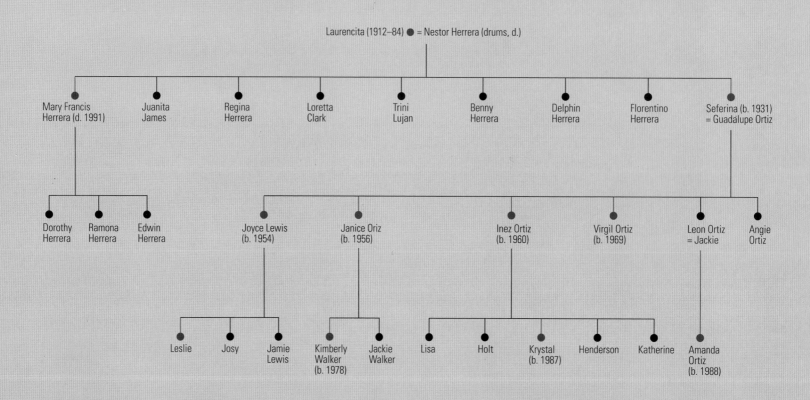

Laurencita (1912–84) ● = Nestor Herrera (drums, d.)

Mary Francis Herrera (d. 1991) — Juanita James — Regina Herrera — Loretta Clark — Trini Lujan — Benny Herrera — Delphin Herrera — Florentino Herrera — Seferina (b. 1931) = Guadalupe Ortiz

Dorothy Herrera — Ramona Herrera — Edwin Herrera — Joyce Lewis (b. 1954) — Janice Oriz (b. 1956) — Inez Ortiz (b. 1960) — Virgil Ortiz (b. 1969) — Leon Ortiz = Jackie — Angie Ortiz

Leslie — Josy — Jamie Lewis — Kimberly Walker (b. 1978) — Jackie Walker — Lisa — Holt — Krystal (b. 1987) — Henderson — Katherine — Amanda Ortiz (b. 1988)

Laurencita Herrera, b. 1912, d. 1984
On Seferina Ortiz: "She was one of a few making traditional pottery. She did all kinds of things: water jars, bowls, and figurines. I think she started the figurines in the 1960s. Just by watching her is how we learned. She would be the main inspiration on my part."

Laurencita Herrera, October 1958 (photographer unknown, courtesy Seferina Ortiz). Pots: left: female figure, height 9¾ in., 1958, IAF 2755, courtesy Indian Arts Research Center, School of American Research, Santa Fe; right: male figure, height 10¾ in., 1958, IAF 2756, courtesy Indian Arts Research Center, School of American Research, Santa Fe.

Seferina Ortiz, b. 1931
"I started making miniatures and gradually I started making larger ones. Now I make pots along with the figurines. I'm doing figures the traditional way. We started reviving the circus people, and we do nativities and I do the 'bathing beauties.' I like making the bears the most. My husband [Guadalupe] makes some, and he's learning to design. I make the black paint from the wild spinach (beeweed) plant. We have to dig the slip—ten to twelve feet underground until we found a layer."

Opposite: Laurencita Herrera. Story-teller, height 5¾ in., ca. 1975, Rick Dillingham inventory.

Seferina Ortiz. Bear figures: left: seated, height 4¾ in., 1992, Rick Dillingham inventory; right: standing, height 4¼ in., 1992, Rick Dillingham inventory.

Virgil Ortiz, b. 1969
"We were asked to revive the older figures, and we had pictures of old pieces. I started researching them and got more pictures. Everything I do is traditional. I still use the same designs, but I'll change them to add my own style. The first one [figure] I made is when I was six years old. I'm experimenting with pots, and I specialize in bears and circus people. I'm trying to revive the standing figures."

Joyce Lewis, b. 1954
"A lot of people wanted little things [pots], so I tried small. It seems I can make them better than big ones. Sometimes I make little tiny storytellers, too."

Joyce Ortiz Lewis. Nativity set, 1993, tallest figure 2 ½ in. Courtesy Seferina Ortiz.

Opposite: Virgil Ortiz. Figure, height 11 in., 1989. Rick Dillingham collection.

Janice Ortiz, b. 1956
"I range in anything from tiny miniature nativity sets to storytellers, plus the ceramics [commercial slipcast ware]. I do pots and mugs and little animals in ceramic. I do a lot of ceramic wedding vases also. I got everything from my mom—I use a lot of her designs. The designs were handed down in the family to the kids. I learned within the past year and a half, and I recently learned to paint with the yucca instead of brushes. I like it better than paint brushes, the lines are straight."

Inez Ortiz, b. 1960
"I make all kinds of things: bears, nativity sets, miniatures, story-tellers, owls, turtles, and clay drums. I mold the 'couple' pieces [a man and woman together] in different sizes. I'm also into the ceramics to make some things easier. I go back to the traditional because people like it."

Opposite: Janice Ortiz. Storyteller, height 5 ½ in., 1992. Rick Dillingham inventory.

Inez Ortiz. Storyteller, height 2 ¾ in., 1992. Rick Dillingham inventory.

Group portrait: (Left to right) top row: Jamie Lewis, Kimberly Walker, Lisa Holt, bottom row: Krystal Henderson, Jackie Walker, and Amanda Ortiz.

SANTO DOMINGO

The Melchor Family

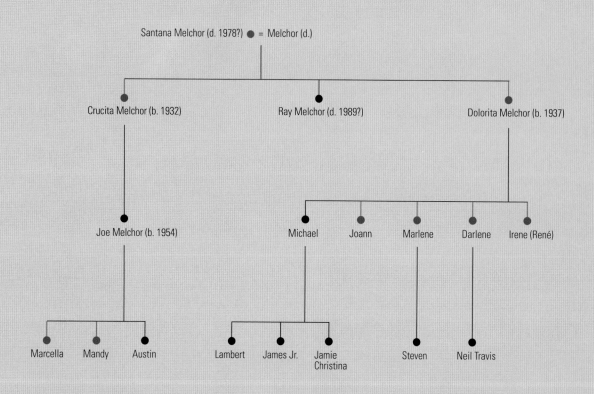

Santana Melchor (d. 1978?) ● = Melchor (d.)

Crucita Melchor (b. 1932)   Ray Melchor (d. 1989?)   Dolorita Melchor (b. 1937)

Joe Melchor (b. 1954)   Michael   Joann   Marlene   Darlene   Irene (René)

Marcella   Mandy   Austin   Lambert   James Jr.   Jamie Christina   Steven   Neil Travis

Santana Melchor (courtesy Crucita and Dolorita Melchor). Pot: flag, 8 x 9 ½ in., 1976, Rick Dillingham collection.

Crucita Melchor, b. 1932
About her mother Santana Melchor: *"She didn't go to school, she stayed home all the time. She was a housewife—cooking, making pottery and jewelry. She did mostly pottery she learned from her mother, Maria Garcia. She made small pots when she was very young, and at around twenty-five years old she was making big storage jars all by herself."*

"I used to do designs when I was eighteen or so—I was still in school—and I'm still doing the painting.

"Its important for me that the kids carry on, because it's been in the family. It's a way to make a living."

Opposite: Santana Melchor. Pot: red birds, 12 ½ x 14 in., ca. 1975. Rick Dillingham collection.

Crucita Melchor. Pot 5 ½ x 13 in., ca. 1987. Rick Dillingham collection.

Dolorita Melchor, b. 1937
"I fill in the blanks after Crucita has outlined the designs. We use old designs, what you see from the old pots."

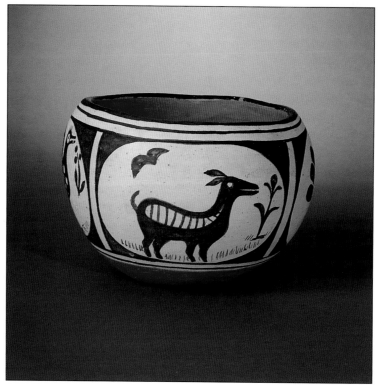

Top: Left: Mandy Melchor (portrait not available). Pot 2 x 3 in., 1986. Middle: Marlene Melchor (portrait not available). Pot 2 ½ x 3 in., 1979. Right: Ilene René Melchor (portrait not available). Pot 2 x 2 ¼ in., 1991. All pots courtesy Crucita Melchor.

Bottom: Dolorita Melchor. Pot made with Crucita Melchor, 5 ¼ x 8 ¼ in., ca. 1987. SAR 1990-16-1, courtesy Indian Arts Research Center, School of American Research, Santa Fe.

Opposite: Dolorita Melchor. Pot made with Crucita Melchor, 6 ¼ x 10 ¼ in., ca. 1988. SAR 1990-16-2, courtesy Indian Arts Research Center, School of American Research, Santa Fe.

The Tenorio Family

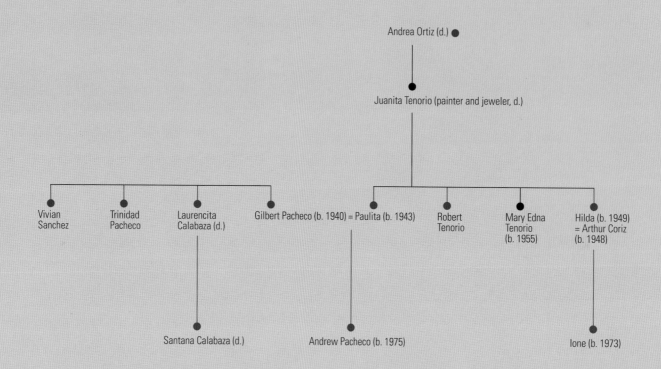

Andrea Ortiz (d.)

Juanita Tenorio (painter and jeweler, d.)

Vivian Sanchez

Trinidad Pacheco

Laurencita Calabaza (d.)

Gilbert Pacheco (b. 1940) = Paulita (b. 1943)

Robert Tenorio

Mary Edna Tenorio (b. 1955)

Hilda (b. 1949) = Arthur Coriz (b. 1948)

Santana Calabaza (d.)

Andrew Pacheco (b. 1975)

Ione (b. 1973)

Gilbert Pacheco, b. 1940, and Paulita Pacheco, b. 1943
Gilbert: "I used to help my mother as a youngster. I was interested in clay and we lived with grandmother in Sile at the ranch and would watch her make pots. We used to make tiny pots for the spirits to give us talent.

"I went through high school and after that I went into the army. Before we were married, Paulita worked with the handicapped at Head Start. After we got married, about five years, we got back together with pottery. It's been about twenty years of making pottery. We started with smaller pots, chili bowls, and sold to people here at the village or Santa Ana or Cochiti for traditional purposes. We started doing shows like Indian Market and we received awards. Now we're doing mostly bowls painted inside. Its all traditional and noncommercial. I do water jars, dough bowls, and pitchers. They went out of style, and now we're doing them.

"Mostly people are doing ceramic. We made two to show people the difference. Together we mix the clay, and we'll decide what we will make. We both form pots, and after they're dry [Paulita] sands and puts on the slip and I do the outlines on the painting [bowl interiors] and she fills them in. We both do the outside painting [bowl exteriors]."

Paulita Pacheco, on her son Andrew Pacheco, b. 1975
"He was going to Head Start and he learned by watching Robert [Tenorio]. He started playing with clay at five years old and at seven years started forming. At nine to ten he started dinosaur designs. It started with a project at school having to do with dinosaurs and he got real interested. We encouraged him to do stories about the pottery designs, and he would write them and put the paper inside the pots. He gives credit for his work to his Uncle Robert."

Previous page: Robert Tenorio (portrait not available). Pot 10 x 9 ½ in., 1987. SAR 1987-8-I, courtesy Indian Arts Research Center, School of American Research, Santa Fe.

Opposite: Paulita and Gilbert Pacheco. Pot 4 ¾ x 13 ¾ in., 1992. Rick Dillingham inventory.

Opposite: Andrew Pacheco. 8 ½ x 8 ½ in., 1990. SAR 1990-16-3, courtesy Indian Arts Research Center, School of American Research, Santa Fe.

Mary Edna Tenorio. Pot 3 x 8 ½ in., painted by Robert Tenorio, 1992. Courtesy Arthur and Hilda Coriz.

Arthur Coriz, b. 1948, and Hilda Coriz, b. 1949

Arthur: "I started making in 1975, nobody taught me how. I just learned by watching Robert [Tenorio] and Hilda. Robert used to paint for me, then a year or two later I started painting my own. I am learning to put on the white [slip]—it's always been Hilda's work. We both do the red [slip] and we both design. I mostly do stew bowls, dough bowls, water jars, and canteens.

"What we do on our pottery is nothing commercial, all is natural—clay, slip paint, and firing. It's all hand made, hand coiled."

Hilda: " My grandmothers both made pottery, and my mother made plain polished black and red pottery. I really learned from Robert, so I give him the credit. We made jewelry before pottery. Mary's been making since around 1983, and she has Robert do the painting. Ione also makes bowls with bird heads and tails."

Opposite: Hilda and Arthur Coriz. Pots: bowl, 2 ¾ x 6 ¼ in., 1992, courtesy of the artists; jar, 6 x 7 in., 1992, courtesy of the artists.

Ione Coriz. Pot 4 x 4 in., 1992. Courtesy Arthur and Hilda Coriz.

SANTA CLARA

The Chavarria Family

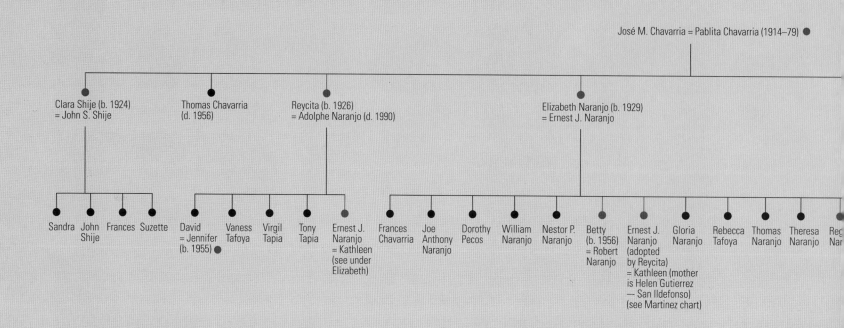

José M. Chavarria = Pablita Chavarria (1914–79)

Clara Shije (b. 1924)
= John S. Shije

Thomas Chavarria
(d. 1956)

Reycita (b. 1926)
= Adolphe Naranjo (d. 1990)

Elizabeth Naranjo (b. 1929)
= Ernest J. Naranjo

Sandra John Shije Frances Suzette

David
= Jennifer
(b. 1955)

Vaness Tafoya

Virgil Tapia

Tony Tapia

Ernest J.
Naranjo
= Kathleen
(see under
Elizabeth)

Frances Chavarria

Joe Anthony Naranjo

Dorothy Pecos

William Naranjo

Nestor P. Naranjo

Betty
(b. 1956)
= Robert
Naranjo

Ernest J.
Naranjo
(adopted
by Reycita)
= Kathleen (mother
is Helen Gutierrez
— San Ildefonso)
(see Martinez chart)

Gloria Naranjo

Rebecca Tafoya

Thomas Naranjo

Theresa Naranjo

Reç
Nar

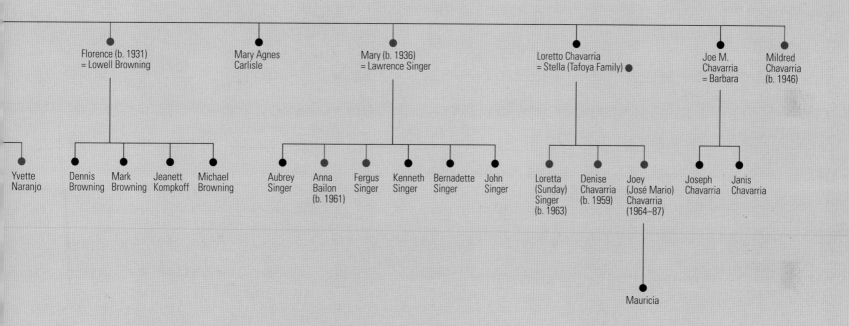

Florence (b. 1931)
= Lowell Browning

Mary Agnes
Carlisle

Mary (b. 1936)
= Lawrence Singer

Loretto Chavarria
= Stella (Tafoya Family)

Joe M.
Chavarria
= Barbara

Mildred
Chavarria
(b. 1946)

Yvette
Naranjo

Dennis
Browning

Mark
Browning

Jeanett
Kompkoff

Michael
Browning

Aubrey
Singer

Anna
Bailon
(b. 1961)

Fergus
Singer

Kenneth
Singer

Bernadette
Singer

John
Singer

Loretta
(Sunday)
Singer
(b. 1963)

Denise
Chavarria
(b. 1959)

Joey
(José Mario)
Chavarria
(1964–87)

Joseph
Chavarria

Janis
Chavarria

Mauricia

Clara Shije, b. 1924
"We all learned it from my mother [Pablita Chavarria]. We were with her all the time and we would watch. Mom passed away in 1979 [b. 1900]. I do baskets, wedding vases, and bowls. The basket handles are hard to do. We [Clara's mother and sisters] used to work together, but now we're on our own. I work sometimes with Florence because it takes two to fire. Everything is done by ourselves. I plan to stay with traditional style. I tried big pots, but decided to stay with smaller pieces."

Opposite: Pablita Chavarria, ca. 1965 (courtesy Elizabeth Naranjo). Pot 14 ¾ x 9 ½ in., ca. 1965. Courtesy Elizabeth Naranjo.

Clara Shije. Pot 5 ½ x 4 ½ in., 1992. Rick Dillingham inventory.

Reycita Naranjo, b. 1926
"The way I learned from my mom is the way I make my pots. I go after my own clay and I pick the big chunks. I pray before I take my clay and the sand I buy from Pojoaque [Pueblo]. I have to dry my clay real good in the sun before I soak them. Then I pound them into small chunks, about an inch, and then dry them in the oven—then they soak better. I sift my clay wet, then I mix the sand. My husband made a sifter out of screen—that's the reason I have no nails!

"I sift my sand and mix it with the clay. It has to be mixed real good, and then I set it out for a day. Then I start molding. I have little dishes for the bases of small ones, then coil them up. I shape them with gourds. I like the twisted handles, they're hard to do. I like the challenge. I only make two twisted-handle wedding vases a day, and I can make four or five bowls a day depending on the size. I've been getting a lot of orders. Since the weather got nice, I got some firing done."

Opposite: Reycita Naranjo. Pot 11 ½ x 6 ¾ in., ca. 1990. Courtesy of the artist.

Jennifer Naranjo, b. 1955
"I learned from Reycita. I'm carrying on what she taught me. My grandmother [Clara Sisneros] influenced me, but I was small when she passed away. My mom is a nurse and I didn't learn [pottery] from her. When I married David, I began to learn from Reycita. I do mostly traditional black and nativity sets. Mine are mostly smaller bowls, two to eight inches. I'm still in that range, I haven't gone to the big ones yet.

"I have done a lot of nativities. I start in the fall for them. Both my daughters do their little pots. My oldest [Melissa] is seventeen, and the little girl [Amanda] is twelve. They're both interested."

Elizabeth Naranjo, b. 1929
"My mom [Pablita Chavarria] was my teacher. I've been making pots 30 to 35 years. I started as a young girl, learning, and after I got married I really got into it. I paid attention to my mom and watched her, and then I would help her when she was older. She wasn't strong enough to polish, so I'd help her. I think you have to have more patience with big pots than little ones. Betty is the only one of my children who is working [with pottery]. I did some redware, but it was hard using the "fill-in" paint. It's different than the slip used for black. You use the same slip on the black [for polishing and filled-in matte areas], and two different ones for the red."

Left: Elizabeth Naranjo. Opposite: Pot 16 x 12 ½ in., ca. 1980. Rick Dillingham collection.

Right: Jennifer Naranjo. Figure (tallest point) 5 ¾ in., ca. 1990. Courtesy Reycita Naranjo.

Betty Naranjo, b. 1956
"I love my work, I love to do it. It gives me enjoyment and pleasure to work with clay. I like to get my hands muddy. It gives me a livelihood to do during the day. I like the baskets [handled bowls], lamp bases, and bowls. Ernestine and Adrian [Betty's children] have begun to learn. I stick to the blackware. We say we will try red, but so far we've stayed with black."

Betty Naranjo. Pot 4 ½ x 3 ¾ in., 1992. Rick Dillingham inventory.

Opposite: Florence Browning. Pot 3 x 4 ¾ in., ca. 1990. Courtesy of the artist.

154

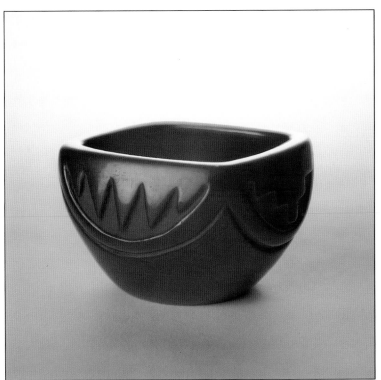

Florence Browning, b. 1931
"I haven't done anything since the market [Indian Market in August]. The last I did, I sold in Taos. I'd rather do pottery than anything else. I have to work, for the Indian Health Service, but am looking forward to retiring so I can work on pottery full-time.

"I sell at the markets. I also sell to dealers. I go to Bandelier every year, usually in the summer for two days. They bring a lot of school children from different states, and I do demos and answer questions. I meet lots of people there and I get to visit.

"Everything I know is from my mother. I started out when I was about ten, and we would fire my little pieces with hers. We're having trouble firing [now]. It's been a bad winter and everything is wet. It's the wind that's the most trouble."

Mildred Chavarria, b. 1946

"I do the medium-sized bowls—I haven't tried anything bigger. I started out seven years ago. I do pottery for income. I don't really go out to shows, I'm not into that. I prefer to make a group of pots and sell them to a dealer. I'm working at the same time [secretary to the Pueblo Governor]. Some people come by the house and I'll sell that way.

"I learned mostly from my mom [Pablita Chavarria], and I watched my sisters and picked it up and took it on my own. The first time was rough, not perfect—but as years have gone by, I'm doing pretty good. I don't think I'll get like my sisters, but my work is good too."

Mary Singer, b. 1936

"I learned from my mom. She's more or less the one who showed me how to make the clay and do polishing. We [my sisters and I] helped her when she was living to fire and do other things with her. She was going to teach us how to do red but we never did. We talked about it, but never did it. She mostly did larger and medium carved black pots. I like large pots, nice large ones where I can work them. I like to go and sell at the markets, but most of the time people call and order. I don't go to Eight Northern [the Indian craft market held in July]—it's too much work. I have gone in the past, but [with Indian Market in Santa Fe in August] it's too much work.

"I try to teach the kids pots. The boy [Fergus] knows how, and I taught my daughter [Anna] how to mix clay. I told them not to rush, do it slowly, you have to do it right from the beginning so they won't bust in the firing.

[About the current trend to kiln fire pottery] "I guess if that's what they want, but they shouldn't call it traditional. I've never seen a kiln."

Opposite: Mary Singer. Pot 14 x 10 in., ca. 1980. Courtesy Wheelwright Museum, Santa Fe.

Mildred Chavarria. Pot 2 ¾ x 4 ½ in., 1993. Rick Dillingham inventory.

The Gutierrez Family

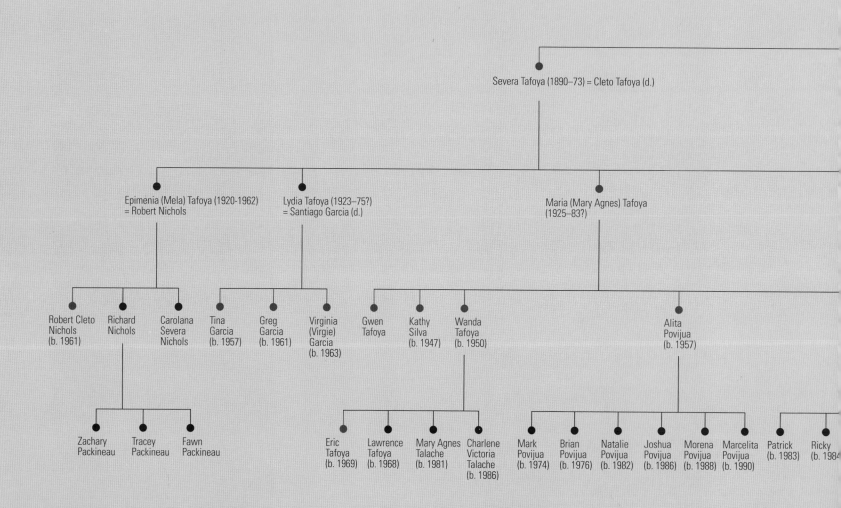

Severa Tafoya (1890–73) = Cleto Tafoya (d.)

Epimenia (Mela) Tafoya (1920-1962)
= Robert Nichols

Lydia Tafoya (1923–75?)
= Santiago Garcia (d.)

Maria (Mary Agnes) Tafoya
(1925–83?)

Robert Cleto
Nichols
(b. 1961)

Richard
Nichols

Carolana
Severa
Nichols

Tina
Garcia
(b. 1957)

Greg
Garcia
(b. 1961)

Virginia
(Virgie)
Garcia
(b. 1963)

Gwen
Tafoya

Kathy
Silva
(b. 1947)

Wanda
Tafoya
(b. 1950)

Alita
Povijua
(b. 1957)

Zachary
Packineau

Tracey
Packineau

Fawn
Packineau

Eric
Tafoya
(b. 1969)

Lawrence
Tafoya
(b. 1968)

Mary Agnes
Talache
(b. 1981)

Charlene
Victoria
Talache
(b. 1986)

Mark
Povijua
(b. 1974)

Brian
Povijua
(b. 1976)

Natalie
Povijua
(b. 1982)

Joshua
Povijua
(b. 1986)

Morena
Povijua
(b. 1988)

Marcelita
Povijua
(b. 1990)

Patrick
(b. 1983)

Ricky
(b. 1984

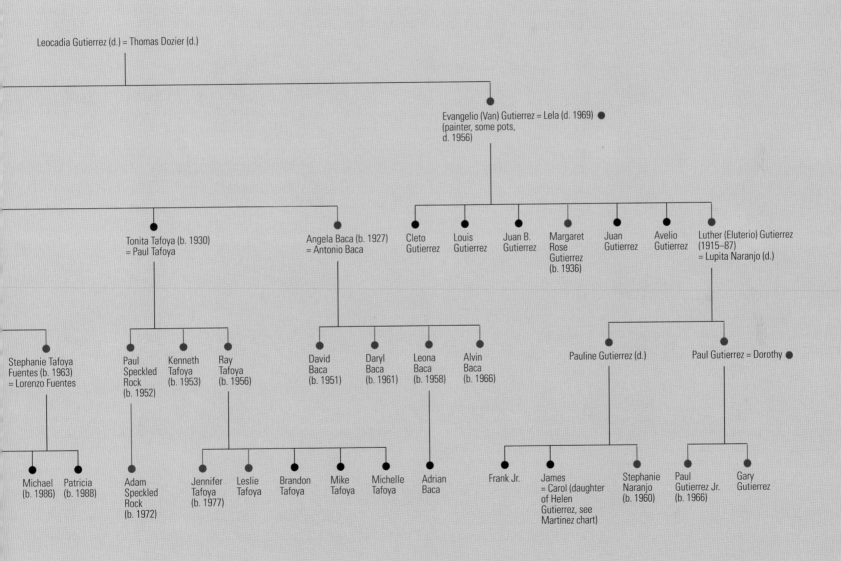

Leocadia Gutierrez (d.) = Thomas Dozier (d.)

Evangelio (Van) Gutierrez = Lela (d. 1969)
(painter, some pots,
d. 1956)

Tonita Tafoya (b. 1930)
= Paul Tafoya

Angela Baca (b. 1927)
= Antonio Baca

Cleto
Gutierrez

Louis
Gutierrez

Juan B.
Gutierrez

Margaret
Rose
Gutierrez
(b. 1936)

Juan
Gutierrez

Avelio
Gutierrez

Luther (Eluterio) Gutierrez
(1915–87)
= Lupita Naranjo (d.)

Stephanie Tafoya
Fuentes (b. 1963)
= Lorenzo Fuentes

Paul
Speckled
Rock
(b. 1952)

Kenneth
Tafoya
(b. 1953)

Ray
Tafoya
(b. 1956)

David
Baca
(b. 1951)

Daryl
Baca
(b. 1961)

Leona
Baca
(b. 1958)

Alvin
Baca
(b. 1966)

Pauline Gutierrez (d.)

Paul Gutierrez = Dorothy

Michael
(b. 1986)

Patricia
(b. 1988)

Adam
Speckled
Rock
(b. 1972)

Jennifer
Tafoya
(b. 1977)

Leslie
Tafoya

Brandon
Tafoya

Mike
Tafoya

Michelle
Tafoya

Adrian
Baca

Frank Jr.

James
= Carol (daughter
of Helen
Gutierrez, see
Martinez chart)

Stephanie
Naranjo
(b. 1960)

Paul
Gutierrez Jr.
(b. 1966)

Gary
Gutierrez

Robert Cleto Nichols, Tall Mountain, b. 1961
"I want to be original with my designs. I got turned off doing the standard feather and serpent designs. I use the melon design, parrot design—a design I came up with—kiva steps, and flowers. I saw a lot of flowers etched [sgraffito] on pottery, and I wanted to incorporate it in my work.

"I learned by watching everybody. It took me a while to learn to mix the clay. I started getting the clay myself. I started part-time when I worked at the Lab [Los Alamos], and what I did didn't come out. The polishing wasn't too hot. [I've been working] maybe since 1987. I'm not looking to be famous or anything, I just want to do it."

Opposite: Severa Tafoya (portrait not available). Pot 6 ¾ x 7 ¾ in., 1961. Courtesy Museum of Indian Art and Culture/Laboratory of Anthropology, Santa Fe.

Robert Cleto Nichols. Pot 4 x 5 ¼ in., 1993. Rick Dillingham inventory.

Virginia Garcia, b. 1963
"I mainly do traditional style because it's more beautiful. My grandmother [Severa Tafoya] started with traditional. My mother [Lydia Garcia] didn't do too much pottery. She did it when I grew up. Tina [Garcia, her sister] caught on, but I didn't get into pottery until 1987, then Tina and my boyfriend encouraged me to work. They kind of pushed, they wanted to see how well I could do. I was messing around at Tina's and she said I should continue. My first pots were pretty bad. I watched the different ways she worked. I work with water jar forms, round bear paw bowls, and wedding vases. I'm starting to get into melon bowls now. I do both black and red, and I don't do carving."

162

Opposite: Virginia Tafoya Garcia. Pot 7 ½ x 5 ¼ in., 1993. Courtesy Povi Jemu Indian Art, Santa Clara Pueblo.

Left: Tina Garcia. Pot 6 x 8 ¼ in., 1993. Courtesy Otowi Trading Company, Santa Fe.

Right: Greg Garcia (portrait not available). Pot 7 ⅛ x 5 ½ in., 1992. Rick Dillingham inventory.

Kathy Silva, b. 1947
"I used to sit with my grandma Severa and my mom used to help her make pottery. We all used to sit together. Severa passed away in 1973. I do the traditional, contemporary and incised [sgraffito].

I do miniatures, regular sizes and larger ones. She [Severa] was a great influence. We got most of our information from her. There are a lot of cousins doing pottery now. I've been potting since I was about six years old. I was teaching Lorenzo [Fuentes] when he married into our family, and his boys."

Wanda Tafoya, b. 1950
"I learned from my grandma, Severa [Tafoya], and took interest from her. My mom [Mary Agnes Tafoya] taught me as well. I do traditional miniatures—that's how I started. After that, we started etching-incised [sgraffito]. I work with my sons Eric and Lawrence. I have a daughter, Mary Agnes—she's one-half Nambe. She's starting to do micaceous pottery [traditional Nambe ware] and traditional Santa Clara. My other daughter, Charlene, is also doing micaceous pottery.

"I do big ones too, seed pots. I did several shows in Scottsdale, Kansas City, Missouri, and Tucson. I hope to do the Indian Market. The family has been doing Indian Market for about 35 years."

Stephanie Tafoya Fuentes, b. 1963
"I basically learned it from my mother [Mary Agnes Tafoya]. She was a potter and Severa's daughter. The pottery I do is mostly incised [sgraffito] type, and I mostly do miniatures. I don't do big ones because it's hard to finish and fire. We [Lorenzo Fuentes, her husband] do animals and flowers and hummingbirds [sculpture].

"I was too young to learn from Severa, and she was up in years at that time. Through my mother and my sisters, I got interested. I'm going to try to continue what I'm doing. I'm doing miniature wedding vases—they're hard. Smaller ones are easier for me. I think people really like the miniatures."

Lorenzo Fuentes [Stephanie Fuentes' husband], b. 1963
"My mother and grandmother are Santa Clara. I was born in California, and when I came back [to Santa Clara], Stephanie said, 'Why don't you try [pottery]?'

"Kathy [Silva] taught me how to get started. Kathy showed me the etching and two-tone firing. [Stephanie and I] have been married 8 years, and she helps me polish now and then. I collect the materials and fire myself. I'll probably go bigger with the pots in the future. I got a Third Place at the Eight Northern this year [1993]."

Alita Povijua, b. 1957
"I do incised [sgraffito] and traditional. I've been potting ten to fifteen years. My main influence was my mom [Mary Agnes Tafoya] and grandma [Severa Tafoya]. I do most the arts and crafts fairs and show my work there. I do some red as well as the black."

Opposite top: Kathy Silva. Pot 2 7/8 x 2 in..

Opposite bottom: Eric Tafoya (portrait not available). Pot 3 1/4 x 3 1/4 in., 1993. Courtesy Povi Jemu Indian Art, Santa Clara Pueblo.

Stephanie Fuentes. Pot 1 7/8 x 1 3/4 in., 1993. Courtesy Povi Jemu Indian Art, Santa Clara Pueblo.

Angela Baca, b. 1927
"I started making with my mother [Severa Tafoya]. She would say, 'Learn to make some, learn to make some, that way when I'm gone you'll know.' We used to live in Paul Speckled Rock's gallery [in the center of the plaza]. She was making a big pot for the Indian Market. 'Here, you polish it,' she said, and that was the first time. She said 'You did good work.' I don't remember what year that was. Then we both worked together. She was awarded a French government award along with Maria [Martinez], and they had to go to Gallup to receive it. Most people don't know about that. Pablita Velarde got one also.

"My mother makes melon bowls with bigger ridges, and one year I told her I'd like to try making them with smaller ridges. A lot of people started making melon bowls. When I started, I got a first prize at Indian Market. They've been making them [melon bowls] here along with the bear paw and black pots— it's Santa Clara traditional pottery. I used to make serpent designs, rain or water serpent.

"My father did all my mother's carving. Severa died in 1973. She was eighty-six. She made pottery up to a couple years before she died."

David Yellow Mountain Baca, b. 1951
"I started—it's about twelve years now. I didn't learn from my mom. I taught myself. My polishing is different from hers. I do traditional and contemporary, black and red. I also do clay peace pipes. The contemporary shapes are different from the traditional. What I'm known for is my squash design melon and seed pot melon. I've won awards at the Eight Northern Pueblos show, Indian Market, Gallup, and the Heard Museum. I got influenced at Eight Northern when it was here at Santa Clara. When I stayed in my mom's booth, people kept asking me questions, and I got into it then. My mom said, 'Why don't you try melons?' I was doing the etching [sgraffito] and contemporary work. Right now, hopefully, I'd like to have my work represented in the Smithsonian."

*Left: Angela Baca. Pot 3 ⅝ x 5 ¼
in., 1993. Courtesy Merrock Galeria,
Santa Clara Pueblo.*

*Right: David Baca. Pot 4 x 4 in., 1993.
Courtesy Povi Jemu Indian Art,
Santa Clara Pueblo.*

Leona Baca, b. 1958
"I was little when I started, ten or twelve years old. I do the exact thing my mom does, only miniatures. I do mostly black, but I do red sometimes. I work full-time [as an electronics technician] and work on weekends and when I find time. The only time I make a lot is for the shows—Eight Northern and Indian Market. Sometimes I have extra ones to sell. When I do make them I have my mother and brothers fire them, and sometimes I don't even see them before they're sold. I used to make bear paw [patterns on pottery forms] when I first started but I haven't made them in a long time. I have a son who is really interested. I guess I'll teach him how to do it."

Top: Leona Baca. Pot 2 x 2 ⅛ in., 1993. Courtesy of the artist.

Bottom: Daryl Baca (portrait not available). Pot 3 x 4 ¾ in., 1993. Courtesy Angela Baca.

Opposite: Alvin Baca. Pot 4 ⅜ x 3 ½ in., 1993. Courtesy of the artist.

Alvin Baca, b. 1966
"I learned from my mom, she taught me how to make pottery. We always sit together and make pots. I didn't know how, and she'd polish my first pots because I would break them. Mine are more like jars and hers are bowls. I don't know where I came up with the shape. I do both black and red. I make canteens too. They're hard to make and I do them for Indian Market. I started a new design with horizontal ridges. They look like a beehive."

Paul Speckled Rock, b. 1952

"My grandmother [Severa Tafoya] was my first inspiration. I made plain bowls and contemporary styles that I like. Of all the different things you can do with the clay, I don't like to stay with only traditional, though I use traditional methods. The bear fetishes I do are important to me. Larger pieces, pottery forms—that's what I'm doing now. I have supported his work [Adam Speckled Rock's], but he learned mostly from his mother [Rosemary Apple Blossom].

"I find selling other people's work [in my gallery] rewarding. I get to learn more about who my customers are. No two people are alike, and all have different tastes. I'd like to see my work in great collections, especially museums."

Paul Speckled Rock. Pot 2 ½ x 2 in., 1991. Courtesy Agape Southwest Pueblo Pottery, Albuquerque.

Opposite: Ray Tafoya. Pot 3 x 5 in., 1992. Courtesy Santa Fe Indian Trading Company, Santa Fe.

Ray Tafoya, b. 1956
"I started out as a silversmith in my teens. I was doing real good in silversmithing. I used to work for my father. He opened a little business doing jewelry. In around 1976 I started playing with clay, and in 1977 I got married to my wife Emily Suazo. She was making pottery. When silver prices went up in 1977, we incorporated our work together and started working in incised [sgraffito] pottery and continue to do so to this day.

"I'm kind of like a perfectionist. I used to work with eyeware and we couldn't make any mistakes because we were working with people's eyes. I applied what I learned to my creativity and firing. I make sure the preparations are just right. It [the firing] is the final judgment, and I don't loose any today. I don't fire a lot at a time, just a few so it's more controlled.

"The black is fired twice, black [firing], then etched [sgraffito], then I apply slips and fire again for a short period to set the slip. The red is fired once, the etching is done, slips applied and fired once.

"I have achieved a lot in my work, but I'm still not satisfied. In pottery the sky's the limit—what you put into it. I express this to my daughters, to do their best. I'm very pleased with what they've done with their art. I've seen interest in all my children to work with clay."

Kenneth Tafoya, b. 1953
"What I used to do was a lot of different shapes with etching [sgraffito]. I still use traditional methods. I used to do wedding vases and seed pots, but what I feel most comfortable with now are the bear figures—I guess you can call them fetishes. We have bears in our mountains here. We Indian people are pushing the bear out of our areas because we are focusing more on the recreation of the mountains. We are having trouble with co-existence. I would like to co-exist and that's why I focus on this creature here. The BIA and Game and Fish people, in order for the bears not to damage the recreation areas, relocate them. I'm not happy with this—they should stay in the mountains. They should leave them be."

Jennifer Tafoya, b. 1977
"I've been working with clay since I was about six. I was making bowls and little polished clay balls with simple designs that were scratched in. I do turtles and lizards and bears once in a while. They are red and black. I think I'll go off in other directions. I'm still learning how to handle the clay. I'm doing my own making, sanding, and polishing, and my dad's teaching me how to fire."

Jennifer Tafoya. (Pot not available).

Opposite: Kenneth Tafoya. Bear fetish, 4 x 10 ½ in., 1993. Courtesy of the artist.

Lela and Van Gutierrez, ca. 1933 (photographer unknown, courtesy Margaret Gutierrez). Pots: opposite: polychrome, ca. 1930, 7 x 7 ½, signed Lela and painted by Van, Rick Dillingham collection; left: black-on-black with orange pigment, 3 ¼ x 6 in. ca. 1930, signed by Lela and painted by Van, Rick Dillingham collection; right: polychrome, 9 ¼ x 9 in., 1932, IAF 1846, courtesy Indian Arts Research Center, School of American Research, Santa Fe .

Margaret Gutierrez, b. 1936

"They [Lela and Van Gutierrez] are the first ones who did the colors. I don't know how they came up with it—I never asked them. I guess by trial and error they came out with these colors—picking out clays and seeing what works and what doesn't work. Mom and Dad worked together, then Luther painted for her [during and after Van's death], and after she passed away I took over. When Pauline was alive she worked by herself. After Luther passed away, I signed the pottery by myself. My dad and Luther overlapped with painting.

"I still travel all over to get clays. I was over to the Grand Canyon and off to Denver. They're the only places I can find what I want. You can find it around here, too—La Bajada, Los Alamos. I go around and pick it up.

"Mom and Dad did some animals, but we just made them up. They didn't do as many as we did. Stephanie is doing figures.

"I'm working, working, working to try to finish some up. I do everything from start to finish now. I still fire outside. I lost a big turtle and wedding vase last week—oh, just crush it up! It's one of these things you have to chance. Now I fire one at a time, and I can pile up the animals, ten or so at a time. You have to get up so early in summer to fire, 4 or 5 a.m. Mostly everybody does the same thing here. Gosh, you can just smell it before the shows. Everybody's trying to do their things!

"Mom and Dad were potting before I was born and before Luther was born. They lost three kids before Luther was born—they had nine kids in all. Luther's kids, Paul and Pauline, were raised by Mom and Dad. We were like triplets."

Margaret Gutierrez. Polychrome pot 3 ¼ x 5 in., 1991. Rick Dillingham inventory.

Opposite: Pot by Margaret and Luther Gutierrez: polychrome, 9 x 9 ½ in., ca. 1970. Rick Dillingham collection.

Opposite: Lela and Luther Gutierrez: polychrome pot, 8 ⅜ in. x 6 in., 1962, signed Lela and Luther (painted by Luther). IAF 2943, courtesy Indian Arts Research Center, School of American Research, Santa Fe. Lela and Luther Gutierrez, August 25, 1963, under the portal at the Palace of the Governors, Santa Fe (photo by Margaret and Paul Peters, courtesy Margaret Gutierrez).

Margaret and Luther Gutierrez: polychrome animal figure, height 4 ⅜ in., ca. 1975, SAR 1989-7-298, courtesy Indian Arts Research Center, School of American Research, Santa Fe.

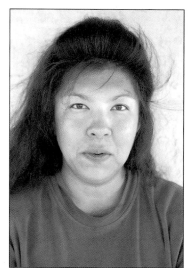

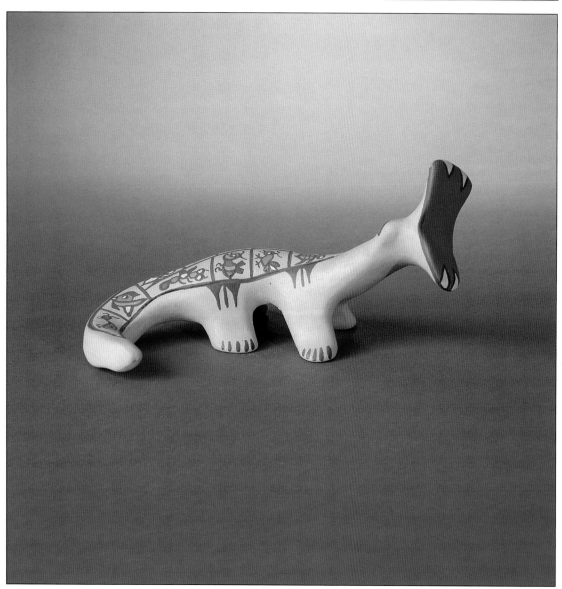

Stephanie Naranjo. Pot 2 ¾ x 6 in. long, ca. 1988. Courtesy Buckner/ Lazarus collection, New York.

Opposite: Pauline Gutierrez, ca. 1985 (photographer unknown, courtesy Margaret Gutierrez). Pot 3 ½ x 5 ¼ in., ca 1987. Courtesy Stephanie Naranjo.

Paul Gutierrez, Sr., b. 1936, and Dorothy, b. 1940, [Navajo]

Paul Sr.: "That's how we make our living mostly. I learned from Margaret and Pauline, but I started with my grandmother [Lela]. But mostly we learned from Pauline and Margaret. We work in black; I don't have the patience to design. We do black and red, mostly figurines.

"Maybe later on we'll do the polychrome. Gary does some, he's a good designer. I'm not a good designer. My grandfather [Van] said he wanted to do polychrome. He went to different places getting colored clay [to make into slips] and see what would stick on pottery.

"Gary does everything alone. He's so picky he doesn't want anyone to monkey around with his pottery."

Dorothy: "We got married in 1965. I watched Pauline and Margaret. My mother is Navajo and makes rugs. We sell in Albuquerque and Santa Fe, Colorado, Arizona, the East, and California, different galleries. We sell at markets and to dealers. It's better to sell to everybody. All I do is make animals and nativities. I make and he [Paul Sr.] sands, polishes, and finishes, and he does the firing."

Paul Gutierrez, Sr.

Opposite: Paul Gutierrez, Jr. Pueblo sculpture, 5 ¾ x 4 in., ca. 1990. Courtesy of the artist.

Paul Gutierrez, Jr., b. 1966
"I watch her [Dorothy, his mother] make animals, mudheads, nativities, shaping the figurines. I haven't really done it seriously, but I want to continue. We used to visit Margaret and Luther, but I learned from my own family. I used to watch my grandfather [Luther] put designs on pots and I'd watch Margaret and Pauline sanding pottery. I do just blackware, like my mom. If you're going to make pottery you've got to be patient and happy with what you're doing."

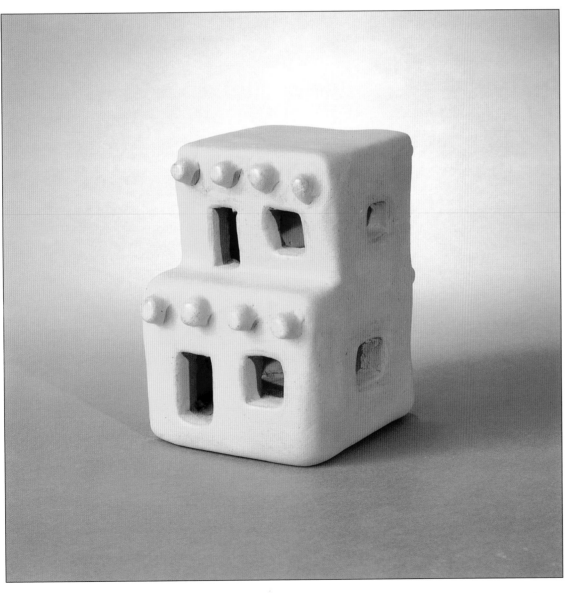

The Tafoya Family

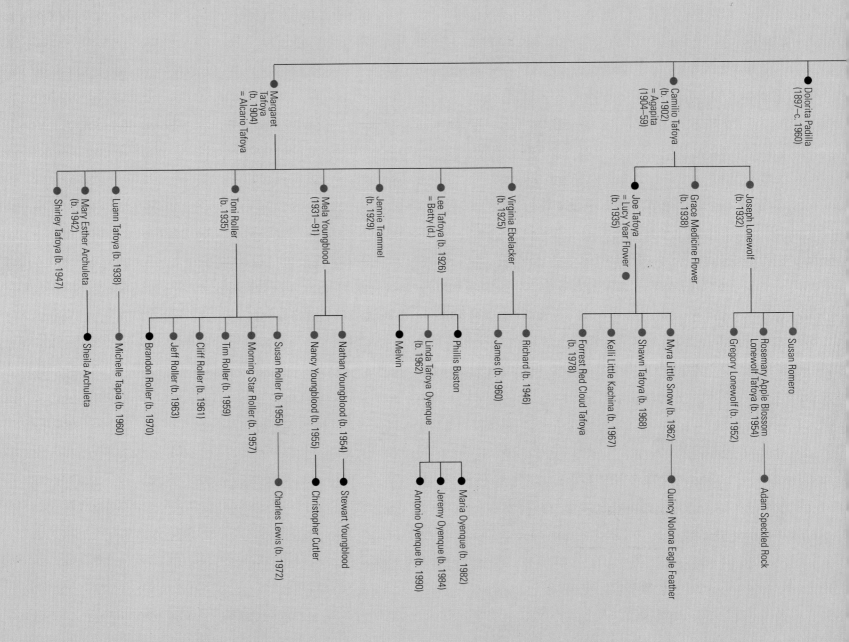

Dolorita Padilla
(1897–c. 1960)

Camilio Tafoya
(b. 1902)
= Agapita
(1904–59)

Margaret
Tafoya
(b. 1904)
= Alcario Tafoya

Shirley Tafoya (b. 1947)

Mary Esther Archuleta
(b. 1942)

Luann Tafoya (b. 1938)

Toni Roller
(b. 1935)

Mela Youngblood
(1931–91)

Jennie Trammel
(b. 1929)

Lee Tafoya (b. 1926)
= Betty (d.   )

Virginia Ebelacker
(b. 1925)

Joe Tafoya
= Lucy Year Flower
(b. 1935)

Grace Medicine Flower
(b. 1938)

Joseph Lonewolf
(b. 1932)

Rosemary Apple Blossom
Lonewolf Tafoya (b. 1954)

Susan Romero

Sheila Archuleta

Michelle Tapia (b. 1960)

Brandon Roller (b. 1970)

Jeff Roller (b. 1963)

Cliff Roller (b. 1961)

Tim Roller (b. 1959)

Morning Star Roller (b. 1957)

Susan Roller (b. 1955)

Nancy Youngblood (b. 1955)

Nathan Youngblood (b. 1954)

Melvin

Linda Tafoya Oyenque
(b. 1962)

Philis Buston

James (b. 1960)

Richard (b. 1946)

Forrest Red Cloud Tafoya
(b. 1978)

Kelli Little Kachina (b. 1967)

Shawn Tafoya (b. 1968)

Myra Little Snow (b. 1962)

Gregory Lonewolf (b. 1952)

Adam Speckled Rock

Charles Lewis (b. 1972)

Christopher Cutler

Stewart Youngblood

Antonio Oyenque (b. 1990)

Jeremy Oyenque (b. 1984)

María Oyenque (b. 1982)

Quincy Nolona Eagle Feather

184

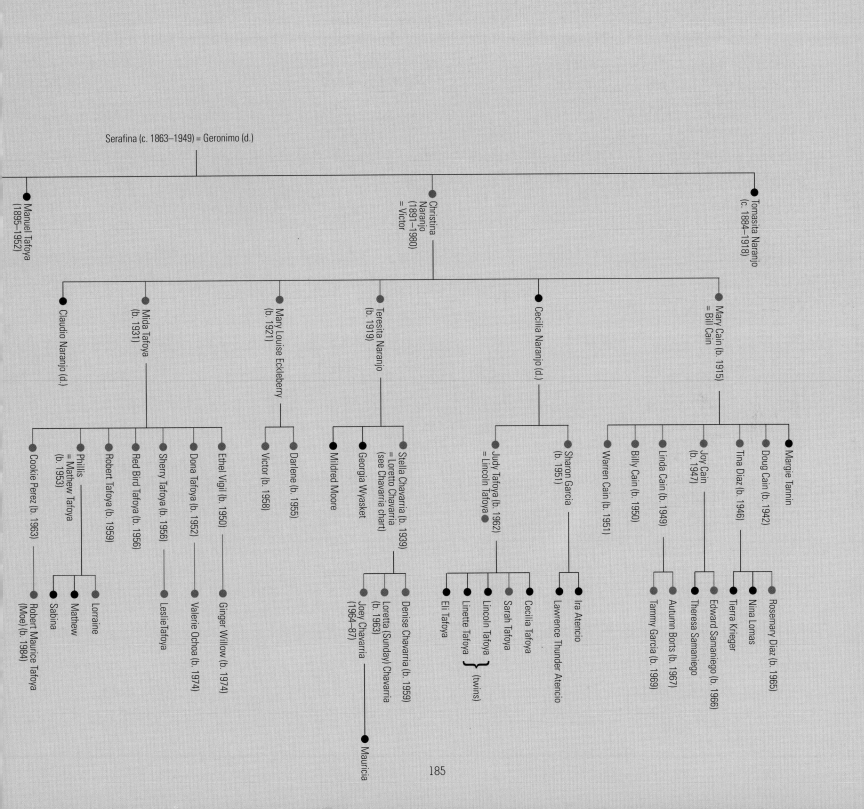

Serafina (c. 1863–1949) = Geronimo (d.)

Manuel Tafoya (1895–1952)

Christina Naranjo (1891–1980) = Victor

Tomasita Naranjo (c. 1884–1918)

Claudio Naranjo (d.)

Mida Tafoya (b. 1931)

Mary Louise Eckleberry (b. 1921)

Teresita Naranjo (b. 1919)

Cecilia Naranjo (d.)

Mary Cain (b. 1915) = Bill Cain

Cookie Perez (b. 1963)

Phillis = Mathew Tafoya (b. 1953)

Robert Tafoya (b. 1959)

Red Bird Tafoya (b. 1956)

Sherry Tafoya (b. 1956)

Dona Tafoya (b. 1952)

Ethel Vigil (b. 1950)

Victor (b. 1958)

Darlene (b. 1955)

Mildred Moore

Georgia Wyasket

Stella Chavarria (b. 1939) = Loretto Chavarria (see Chavarria chart)

Judy Tafoya (b. 1962) = Lincoln Tafoya

Sharon Garcia (b. 1951)

Warren Cain (b. 1951)

Billy Cain (b. 1950)

Linda Cain (b. 1949)

Joey Cain (b. 1947)

Tina Diaz (b. 1946)

Doug Cain (b. 1942)

Margie Tannin

Robert Maurice Tafoya (Moe) (b. 1984)

Sabina

Mathew

Lorraine

Leslie Tafoya

Valerie Ochoa (b. 1974)

Ginger Willow (b. 1974)

Joey Chavarria (1964–87)

Loretta (Sunday) Chavarria (b. 1963)

Denise Chavarria (b. 1959)

Eli Tafoya

Linette Tafoya

Lincoln Tafoya

} (twins)

Sarah Tafoya

Cecilia Tafoya

Lawrence Thunder Atencio

Ira Atencio

Tammy Garcia (b. 1969)

Autumn Borts (b. 1967)

Theresa Samaniego

Edward Samaniego (b. 1966)

Tierra Krieger

Nina Lomas

Rosemary Diaz (b. 1965)

Mauricia

185

Sarafina (Sara Fina or Serafina) Tafoya. Portrait: Geronimo and Sarafina Tafoya courtesy Mary Fredenburg and Lawrence and Mary Ellen Black. Pots: redware, ca. 1925, 4 x 10 in., courtesy Buckner/Lazarus collection, New York; opposite: blackware, 7 ¾ x 10 ¾ in., ca. 1922–23, IAF 2674, courtesy Indian Arts Research Center, School of American Research, Santa Fe.

Margaret Tafoya (portrait not available). Pots: opposite: redware wedding vase, 15 x 11 in., 1982; blackware, 7 1/4 x 9 1/2 in., 1976. Both Rick Dillingham collection.

The following is a statement prepared by Toni Roller, Mary Esther Archuleta, Virginia Ebelacker, Jennie Trammel, LuAnn Tafoya, and their mother Margaret Tafoya, February 1993.

"The Margaret Tafoya family did not wish to be included in the new or revised Seven Families in Pueblo Pottery, in protest against Indian potters who are using commercial materials in making pottery and firing in controlled kilns. We want to inform the public that this is going on while many claim their pottery is traditional. Being published in a book next to this type of potter shows our condoning that kind of work.

"There is room for every kind of potter, but they must specify that their work is nontraditional if they do not use natural materials or do not fire their pottery outdoors. We feel that when an Indian potter falsely presents his work to the public, it is outright fraud. The Tafoya family potters do not claim to be perfect, but we want to do our best to preserve our Indian culture and traditions."

Mary Esther Archuleta (portrait not available). Pot 4 ½ x 7 ½ in., ca. 1988. Courtesy Dewey Galleries, Ltd., Santa Fe.

Opposite: Toni Roller (portrait not available). Pot 9 ½ in. diameter, 1979. Rick Dillingham collection.

Opposite: Jeff Roller (portrait not available). Pot 4 ¼ x 5 ½ in., 1991. Courtesy Case Trading Post/Wheelright Museum, Santa Fe.

Cliff Roller (portrait not available). Pot 4 x 5 ½ in., 1989. Rick Dillingham collection.

Left: Tim Roller (portrait not available). Pot 2 x 3 ½ in., 1992. Courtesy Toni Roller.

Right: Charles Lewis (portrait not available). Pot 4 ½ x 5 ¼ in., 1992. Rick Dillingham inventory.

Opposite: LuAnn Tafoya (portrait not available). Pot 16 x 14 ¼ in., 1992. Courtesy Case Trading Post/Wheelright Museum, Santa Fe.

Jennie Trammel (portrait not available). Pots: opposite: redware, 13 ½ x 9, ca. 1988, courtesy Dewey Galleries, Ltd., Santa Fe; bottom: blackware, 6 x 4 in., 1990, courtesy Case Trading Post/Wheelwright Museum, Santa Fe.

Top: Shirley Tafoya (portrait not available). Pot 2 ¾ x 3 ½ in., 1984. Rick Dillingham collection.

Top left: Lee and Betty Tafoya (Betty is deceased) (portrait not available). Pot 4 x 6 in., 1988. Courtesy Dewey Galleries, Ltd., Santa Fe.

Top right: Linda Tafoya Oyenque (portrait not available). Pot 5 ½ x 4 in., 1991, Rick Dillingham inventory.

Bottom left: Virginia Ebelacker (portrait not available). Pot 6 x 12 ½ in., ca. 1978. Rick Dillingham collection.

Bottom right: James Ebelacker (portrait not available). Pot 8 ½ x 8 ½ in., ca. 1988. Courtesy Buckner/Lazarus collection, New York.

Opposite: Richard Ebelacker (portrait not available). Pot 19 ¾ x 22 ½ in., 1992. Courtesy Museum of Indian Art and Culture/Laboratory of Anthropology, Santa Fe.

Nathan Youngblood, b. 1954
"Where I am right now, it's not easy to stay within traditional boundaries and challenge yourself. I get a lot of feedback from people who say, 'Why do you fire that way [traditional outdoor firing]? Why don't you fire in a kiln? Why do you prepare your clay? Why don't you go to the store and buy it? I guess the reason I don't want to go down that road is because when I lived with my grandparents [Margaret and Alcario Tafoya], the one thing they constantly tried to instill in me was that the way we do our pottery, the traditional way, was the way that was handed to us by the spirits that come before us. In order to show the proper respect for the clay and to the clay we need to continue doing it in the old way, and that means digging your own clays and mixing them together, hand-coiling, hand-burnishing, and outdoor firing."

Opposite: Mela Youngblood (portrait not available). Pot 8 ¾ x 7 ½ in., ca. 1988. Courtesy Dewey Galleries, Ltd., Santa Fe.

Nathan Youngblood. Pot 2 ½ x 11 in., 1988. Courtesy Buckner/Lazarus collection, New York.

Nancy Youngblood, b. 1955

"Everything's changed from when that book [Seven Families] was done. My career has advanced a lot. To some degree, winning ribbons at fairs got me motivated. Sometimes people who collect the work feel that it's important, it points them to an artist—and that's what it did for me. But after so many ribbons it's become less important. I've gotten the acknowledgment I've wanted. On any given day, awards could be given out differently. It's a matter of someone's taste.

"Could I live with this piece? Does it look good to me? That's when I realized what was important.

"I give Margaret Tafoya acknowledgment, that she was a major inspiration to me—not just her work, things like having faith. She would say, 'If you do the right thing, everything will turn out right.'

"Some ideas I've had stored in my mind for many years. Ideas I didn't think I could do. My brother [Nathan Youngblood] was a great inspiration. He said all that was limiting me was my mind, and if you can dream it you can make it. I have to challenge myself or I get lazy and repeat the same things. Another thing that is important to me is different cultures being remembered by their art. I wanted to be remembered for doing something rather than just taking up space in the world. I think of someone a hundred years from now thinking, 'Who was that? How did she do that?'"

Opposite: Nancy Youngblood. Pot 4 x 6 in., 1992. Courtesy Joe Accardo and Maureen McCarthy, Santa Fe.

Joseph Lonewolf, b. 1932
[From a prepared written statement:]
"My creativity, which is inspired by both my parents and the artistic heritage of my People—the Pueblo Indians—intertwines the traditional procedures used by ancestral potters with contemporary methods; and thus, it enables me to perfect my own individual style and means for personal expression. My teachings and our heritage of pottery making continues, today, in the creations of my three children and grandson."

Opposite left: Agapita Tafoya (portrait not available). Pot 4 ¼ x 6 in., ca. 1950. Courtesy Grace Medicine Flower, Santa Clara Pueblo.

Camilio Tafoya (portrait not available). Pots: Opposite top left: 1 ¾ x 1 ¾ in., 1991, courtesy Andrews Pueblo Pottery, Albuquerque; opposite right: 3 ½ x 4 ½ in., 1977, courtesy Grace Medicine Flower, Santa Clara Pueblo.

Joseph Lonewolf, ca. 1987 (photograph by Katheryn M. Favorite, courtesy the photographer, Santa Clara Pueblo). Pots: opposite top right: 1 ¾ x 1 ½ in., 1992, courtesy Andrews Pueblo Pottery, Albuquerque; 3 x 3 ½ in., 1977, SAR 1989-7-286, courtesy Indian Arts Research Center, School of American Research, Santa Fe.

Left: Susan Romero (portrait not available). Pot 2 x 1 ¾ in., 1991. Courtesy Andrews Pueblo Pottery, Albuquerque.

Middle: Rosemary Apple Blossom Lonewolf (1992, photographer unknown). Pot 2 ¾ x 2 ¼ in., 1981. Courtesy Buckner/Lazarus collection, New York.

Right: Gregory Lonewolf. Pot 1 ⅜ x 1 ⅛ in., 1992. Courtesy Andrews Pueblo Pottery, Albuquerque.

Rosemary Apple Blossom Tafoya, b. 1954

[Concerning her recent story-pots] "[They] serve to reflect my personal and unique life experiences. Subject matter ranges from (1) thoughts about a woman's body as a bearer of life, (2) my own pregnancy, (3) feelings about my mixed heritage, (4) what it means to live in the East as a Pueblo Indian, (5) reflections on the Columbus Quincentennary, and (6) even space exploration. In essence, I'm a modern Mimbres, commenting on my twentieth-century world just as those ancient potters did in illustrating their pots with vignettes of daily life. In summary, the themes of my pots are a unique blend of contemporary subjects based on traditional values."

[From the artist's printed statement:] "I am not, nor are my pieces, frozen in time. I am a contemporary Pueblo Indian woman facing complex issues in a rapidly changing world. Sometimes these issues present conflicts to 'traditional' Pueblo life. More often than not, however, the issues are the same personal and professional challenges any modern woman faces. It is these issues, then, that are explored and illustrated as the subject matter of my pots."

Gregory M. Lonewolf, b. 1952

"The first time I remember doing anything with clay and keeping it was a rolled slab of commercial clay in school with an imprint of my hand. My mother still has it.

"The whole family has been working on pottery a long time. I've always been interested in art, but other career things kept me from it until later when I worked in a frame shop and saw artwork coming in. My interest was heightened by talking to these artists and helping them with their work. I thought I'd give it a shot and see if I could sell my own work—etching, glass etching, woodwork, all sorts of media—I was never restricted by that.

"In 1984–85 I did my first show and sold three pieces. Within six months I decided to do this [artwork] full time. I do other artwork than just pottery.

"I got to see a lot of my father's work, but the first teaching I received was from Camilio [Tafoya, his grandfather] and Aunt Grace [Medicine Flower], and we did the traditional carved style. My 'internship' came from my father and sister Rosemary [Apple Blossom]. I learned a lot of different techniques from each member of the family and incorporated these methods into what I do now. I consider my father my mentor and hope someday to catch up with him, but I doubt I will."

[With regard to contemporary innovation at Santa Clara] "If you look at history with the Aztec, Inca, and in China, there was a period of time where the ruling party said, 'This is the way it will be.' Nothing changed, the creativity was stifled. To be a true artist you are always trying new things—from Indian or non-Indian sources. Sometimes you're able to incorporate it into your work. You're like a child, everything is new everyday."

Grace Medicine Flower, b. 1938
[I asked what had changed since the Seven
Families book:]
"Nothing's really changed except the age."

"I did sgraffito only in the seventies, and now I'm
combining deep carving and sgraffito. I'm also
doing bigger pots. I'm doing 'cut-outs' or 'sculp-
tured rims'—I don't have a name for it. I did some
work with my dad when I broke my wrist. He
works mostly with Joseph [Lonewolf]. He doesn't do
much anymore. He'll be ninety this year.

"You gotta change someways—the change has to
be. There are young ones with new ideas and you
have to look. Even traditional work is OK for going
off and doing new things. It makes the art exciting.
The traditional designs are kept, but you can
express in the way you design. If every so many
years you can come up with new ideas, it's exciting
to show them. Some galleries help artists do better
by pushing their work. You can repeat designs, but
they're never the same. I still enjoy it. I guess they
[Agapita and Camilio Tafoya] were making pottery before I was born. Mom used to do painted
pottery on red. Camilio later did carved pottery
and horse sculptures. Agapita passed away in
1959."

Grace Medicine Flower. Opposite: by
Grace Medicine Flower and Camilio
Tafoya, 1971, 4 ¼ x 5 ¼ in., courtesy
Buckner/Lazarus collection, New
York.

Quincy Tafoya, b. 1983
"I make turtles, dinosaurs, reptiles, snakes, bear, rabbits. I do them like Shawn [Tafoya]—red and white—and sometimes I do black. Black's too hard. I'm going to stick with pottery as I get older and do bigger and better ones."

Grace Medicine Flower. Pots left: 3 x 4 ¼ in., 1990, courtesy Andrews Pueblo Pottery, Albuquerque; right: 3 x 3 ¼ in., ca. 1975, courtesy Dewey Galleries, Ltd., Santa Fe.

Quincy Tafoya. Pot not available.

Opposite: Lucy Year Flower Tafoya. Pot 2 ¼ x 3 ½ x 3 in., ca. 1989. Courtesy Buckner/Lazarus collection, New York.

Lucy Year Flower Tafoya, b. 1935
"I started in 1972. I picked it up from Camilio [Tafoya], but consider myself self-taught. I learned to mix the clay myself, and all the pots popped until I got the mixture right. I started with animals, then to little bowls. I did miniatures for a while, and now I'm doing much larger work. I taught my daughters. When I was working, they would play with the clay. Before I knew it, they were making pots. They started getting more and more interested. It helps Myra, because she doesn't have to go to work. Kelli works all the time on pottery."

Myra Little Snow (portrait not available). Pot 3 x 3 ¾ in., 1992. Rick Dillingham inventory.

Christina Naranjo, ca. 1973 (photographer unknown, courtesy Mida Tafoya). Opposite: pot 13 ¾ x 11 ½ in., ca. 1975. Rick Dillingham collection.

Forrest Red Cloud Tafoya, b. 1978
"I was nine or ten when I got started. Shawn was my main teacher. I do the red and white type and I did some turtles in black. My favorite thing to draw on the pots are animals, dinosaurs, dogs, snakes."

Shawn Tafoya, b. 1968
"My work is different because I want to do something different than the usual Santa Clara carved ware. Right now I'm doing red and buff, and I want to go to the older style, Tewa Polychrome, and use it as an inspiration for new work and different designs. My mother [Lucy Year Flower] and aunt, Grace Medicine Flower, were my teachers. They really influenced me. I did blackware when I was younger. I started experimenting with white slip when I was twelve or thirteen, and it took a while to figure out how to do it. It takes a longer, hotter fire than the black."

Opposite: Shawn Tafoya. Pot 6 x 9 in., 1993. Courtesy of the artist.

Top: Forrest Red Cloud. Pot 2 ¼ x 2 ½ in., 1992. Courtesy Buckner/Lazarus collection, New York.

Bottom: Kelli Little Kachina (portrait not available). Pot 4 x 3 ½ in., 1992. Rick Dillingham inventory.

Mary Cain, b. 1915
"I guess mostly it [pottery making] came from my mother [Christina Naranjo]. When my grandmother [Serafina Tafoya] was living I was very young, and she would talk to us about it. When you're very young, you don't want to stay with it. When I started making later with my mom, I didn't want to stop. I started maybe in the late 1930s or early forties and signed some of them Mary Tafoya. We went to California from 1956 to 1973 and I went back and forth and worked with pottery because I wanted to stay with it. In the early 1970s I worked again with my mom.

"I don't want to leave the work. I just love to do it. It makes you feel so good—you're doing something for yourself, not dependent on others. It makes you feel happy.

"Later on, when the kids all came back out here [Santa Clara], I asked if they were interested in pottery and each started and now they're all 'in it.' After they got started, they got real interested and still do it."

Joy Cain, b. 1947
"When I first started, I didn't know anything. I just helped my mom [Mary Cain] and grandmother [Christina Naranjo]. I did all the dirty jobs for them, and then I got started learning from the bottom up. I made little, crooked, tiny bowls and threw most of them away. I learned the polishing from my mom, and heard, 'Do it over,' plenty of times. You've got to have a good stone to do the polishing. Now, I like to work on big bowls—they're a lot more fun. I enjoy the carving the best. It's like a big canvas, your bowl—draw on it and carve it out."

Top left: Joy Cain. Pot 4 ⅝ x 6 ¼ in., 1993. Courtesy of the artist.

Top right: Mary Cain. Opposite: Pot 9 x 7 ¼ in., 1992. Rick Dillingham inventory.

Edward Samaniego (Sunburst), b. 1966
"I like that it's passed down from generation to generation, and it shouldn't be lost. Knowing that fact will inspire me to make pottery, or to work on pottery every day. I like the water jar shape and I like the serpent design. I see great things to come with my art. I also paint in acrylic and oil. [Pottery and painting] are two separate types of art. I stick to the more traditional in pottery, and in the painting I can do anything."

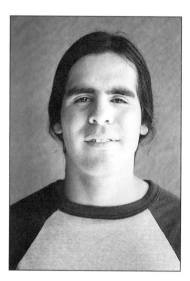

Edward Samaniego. Pot 4 x 4 ½ in., 1992. Courtesy of the artist.

Opposite left: Warren Cain (courtesy Mary Cain). Pot 3 x 5 in., 1993. Rick Dillingham inventory.

Opposite right: Doug Cain (portrait not available). Pot 3 ¼ x 5 ½ in., 1992. Courtesy of the artist.

Tina Diaz, b. 1946
"I feel really proud and fortunate to be a part of this tradition that's being carried on. I love the clay, the people, the whole thing—especially the good-will."

RoseMary Diaz, b. 1965
"Although I am not a potter myself, being part of a family of potters has greatly influenced my work as a writer. I often incorporate certain aspects of pottery making into my writing—the dampness of the clay, the grit of the sand, the smell of the smoke when the pots are fired, and the smooth feel of their shiny surfaces when they're finished. In this way, and through the hands of my mother and her mother, I am connected to the clay."

Bill Cain, b. 1950

"Ten years ago my mother called me and asked if I wanted to learn pots. I was living in California at the time. She taught me how to mix the clay, make [the pottery], slip it, polish it, and fire it. It inspires one a lot, it relaxes me—it takes the tension away. I follow traditional design and add some contemporary. I can get inspired by the designs in the clouds. I like trying different types of clay for different colors. I do the serpent, bear paw, and whatever comes to mind."

Opposite left: RoseMary Diaz (photograph by Paul Keliiaa, 1993). Pot not available.

Opposite right: Tina Diaz. Pot 7 ½ x 4 ½ in., 1991. Rick Dillingham inventory.

Billy Cain. Pot 10 in. dia., 1992. Courtesy of the artist and Mary Cain.

Autumn Borts, b. 1967
"I'm happy to know the ways of the Santa Clara people. I like to create unusual and traditional shapes that my mom [Tina Diaz], grandmother [Mary Cain], and other relatives have taught and shown me. I'm inspired by Mother Earth and the things that happen in life and the things around me."

Top left: Autumn Borts. Pot 8 x 3 ½ in., 1992. Rick Dillingham inventory.

Top right: Linda Cain. Opposite: Pot 6 x 7 ¼ x 3 ¾ in., 1992. Courtesy of the artist.

Tammy Borts Garcia, b. 1969
"I've had a lot of inspiration from the older potters—and [then] mixing it with my own style. I'd say my style was traditional motifs with contemporary shapes. I learned from my mom [Linda Cain] and my grandmother [Mary Cain]. I want to continue doing pottery for as long as I live. I enjoy what I do, working with my hands. My main drive is that I really enjoy it. I enjoy working with the earth and using my mind to create new and different things."

Judy Tafoya, b. 1962
"I used to make small figurines when I was a child. I don't remember anything being finished. Then I left the pueblo when I was fourteen and I didn't return until I was twenty-one. I returned in 1983. My sister Sharon [Garcia] introduced me back into pottery making and helped me get my first pieces done. She helped me and my husband Lincoln Tafoya do our polishing and firing.

"I do traditional carved black pottery. I enjoy making nativity sets. I like to make pots that show something out of the normal. I like to make lidded pots, something I just started in the past year. I like to make the large storage vases.

"My carving is a little different than the rest of the family. I can spot my aunt's and cousin's work by their carving. I learned to create my own style. I didn't have anyone teach me to put the design on. I learned it myself, maybe from memory from when I was young.

"I believe the talent I have is a God-given talent. I'm able to be home with my children and to provide a good living. My husband is also a full-time potter. Lincoln does wildlife designs on his. It's a big responsibility to raise children and be there for them."

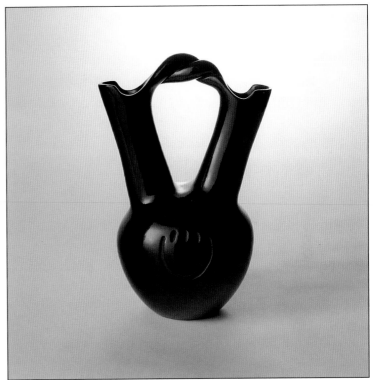

Left: Tammy Garcia. Pot 6 x 5 in.,
1992. Rick Dillingham inventory.

Right: Judy Tafoya. Pot 11 ½ x 7 ¾
in. across spouts, 1993. Courtesy of
the artist.

Sharon Naranjo Garcia, b. 1951
"I learned, of course, from my grandmother [Christina Naranjo]. She raised me. I admired her shapes and her traditional work. I like the water jar with bear paw, the double shoulder, there are many variations. I enjoy the traditional shapes and styles. I do everything by myself. I live in San Juan but continue to work in the Santa Clara style. My boys are picking it up now."

Left: Sharon Garcia. Pot 8 ¼ x 6 ¾ in., 1993. Courtesy Merrock Galeria, Santa Clara Pueblo.

Right: Teresita Naranjo. Pot 7 x 10 in., ca. 1965, IAF 3019. Courtesy Indian Arts Research Center, School of American Research, Santa Fe.

Teresita Naranjo, b. 1919 ("I think I'm 1,000 years old!")
"I used to tell Stella [Chavarria], look at the polishing, that's what shows. Don't work for money, work for a name."

[From a printed paper she prepared] *"I was born and raised in Santa Clara Pueblo and have lived there all my life. My parents were Victor and Christina Naranjo. I was born on May 1, 1919. On the fourth day I was given my Indian name by a midwife, she named me Bay-Po-Vi, which means Apple Blossom: then later on they baptized me in the Catholic Church and gave me my name Teresita Naranjo.*

"I did not know my grandparents on my father's side, they were dead before I was born, but on my mother's side my grandparents were Geronimo and Sarafina Tafoya. They have always done potteries all their lives. Of course, my grandfather was a very good farmer: he always raised his own crops and was always busy in the daytime, but when his work was done he would always do pottery work in the evenings to help my grandmother.

"My grandfather used to tell us the story about the waterdragon, which is called Avanyu in Tewa language which was spoken in his days. However the way he told it was the waterdragon brought luck, health, peace, joy, and happiness as well as rain and good crops to the Indian people and to all people on the earth. So he said whoever buys your pottery with the waterdragon design, he too will always have all those good things.

"Some people may say pottery making is a hobby; it is more than a hobby, thank God. It means my life. I have a business right in my home. I work to make a living. I have supported my children with pottery and given them their education and their needs since my husband died in 1950. Today my pottery means the handiwork of God."

Stella Chavarria, b. 1939
"I've been doing pots about thirty to thirty-two years. My two girls are both working on pots now, and one granddaughter and Joey [d. 1987] used to work. Mauricia is Joey's daughter, and at nine years old she is doing small ones. I learned from watching my mom [Teresita Naranjo] and used most of her traditional designs and those of my grandmother Christina. I enjoy working on pots, and I work every day. I wouldn't do anything else besides this."

Denise Chavarria, b. 1959

"I've been doing it for about twelve years, and it's been full time. It's still full time. I enjoy trying different shapes. I used to do small ones, and now I work a little bigger. My designs are different from my mom [Stella Chavarria] and sister [Loretta]. I learned it all from Mom, and I had to pay her—what—$50 per class! I hope it will make us as well known as my mom. We enjoy going to the different shows."

Opposite: Stella Chavarria. Pot 4 ½ x 3 ½ in., 1991. Rick Dillingham inventory.

Denise Chavarria. Pot 4 ½ x 3 ¾ in., 1992. Rick Dillingham inventory.

Left: Joey Chavarria (portrait not available). Pot 3 ½ x 3 ⅜ in., ca. 1983. Courtesy Otowi Trading Co., Santa Fe.

Middle: Loretta (Sunday) Chavarria. Pot 3 ¼ x 3 ¼ in., 1992. Rick Dillingham inventory.

Right: Mida Tafoya. Pot 3 ¼ x 7 in., ca. 1989. Courtesy Dewey Galleries, Ltd., Santa Fe.

Loretta (Sunday) Chavarria, b. 1963
"I seriously started about four to five years ago. Last year I started doing the etched [sgraffito], and I still do the carved. I watched my mom and learned from her. I mostly work on small ones. I guess I never really tried big ones— smaller ones are easier for me. I also have a full-time job at Los Alamos. I'm a computer operator there."

Mida Tafoya, b. 1931
"I love working with clay. Mother Earth—she's been good to me. To me, pottery making means a lot. Mother Earth never let me down. Whatever I make, wedding vases, bowls, all come out good. I enjoy working with you [referring to unfinished pottery on the table], and people will be happy to have the pots in their homes.

"I enjoy doing shows. I enjoy meeting people and talking about the pottery. I let them touch the clay so they can feel how it is. It's been around thirty years of work, and I learned from Christina [Naranjo]. Me and her used to work together. She showed me how to make pottery, talk with Mother Earth and be good to her—not to be mad—talk to her, how to mold the clay, how to make big ones and take care of myself and the clay.

"My son Robert and his girlfriend do painted red pottery, and he does a lot of small carved ones which he learned from me. My son Mike does the carving like me. Him and his wife work together. She does the polishing, she's from San Ildefonso. He also learned from me. Donna does pottery too, and she works for Pojoaque Pueblo but still helps me with pottery. She does some on her own, but works mostly with me."

[Grandson Robert Maurice (Moe) Tafoya (b. 1984), son of daughter Cookie, said while I was there: "Grandma, can I make a pottery?"]

Phyllis M. Tafoya, b. 1953
"I started making pottery when I was about twelve, and I learned from my grandmother Christina Naranjo and grandmother Lucaria Tafoya. I first started making animals and bowls that had painted designs. The next step I took was making medium-size bowls that were carved. I hung in that area when I was in college. It was after college that I started on my own, my own direction. Now I'm working on traditional black wedding vases and traditional red bowls. I guess I could say I came from little pieces to big stuff. I'm more comfortable making large pots now. With my boyfriend, we make contemporary stuff. I make the bowl and he does the sgraffito design. I'm doing a lot of contemporary . . . they are traditional black and red but use sgraffito design. They are dance pieces with buffalo and deer dancers."

Opposite: Phyllis Tafoya. Pot 9 x 10 ½ in., 1993. Courtesy of the artist.

Sherry Tafoya (portrait not available). Pot 7 ⅞ x 5 ¼ in., 1993. Courtesy Merrock Galeria, Santa Clara Pueblo.

Ethel Vigil, b. 1950
"I take great pride in putting out quality pieces. I sign them, and what I have my name on I want to be proud of. I take great pride in doing the work. It's a money-making thing, but it's also a handed-down art that we learn. I do the red and the black carved pottery. I learned on my own. My mother [Mida Tafoya] did it, and I watched her. I picked it up because I was interested. My work is different from my mother's. I'm trying to teach my four daughters, but the patience isn't there for them yet."

Dona Tafoya, b. 1952
"It's a good source of income. It's extra income, and it also gives you a satisfaction that you can do something with your hands that someone else can appreciate. I don't do it as much now because I have a full-time job—mostly for shows and special events. My mother [Mida Tafoya] and grandmother [Christina Naranjo] were my main teachers."

Cookie Tafoya, b. 1963
"I grew up with it [pottery], watching my grandmother [Christina Naranjo]. I would go to her house after school and cut newspapers to put in her bowls to start pottery. As I got older, I watched my mom. She taught me to polish, carve, and design. My mom basically taught me, and then I developed my own designs—which is important to me because you have your own personality and I like to show mine. I don't like to use the same designs and shapes over and over; I like to try new things. It depends on my mood. Sometimes I can be real creative and sometimes I go with more traditional pots: wedding vases, water pots, and seed pots."

Opposite: Ethel Vigil. Pot 4 ¾ x 3 ½ in., 1993. Courtesy Merrock Galeria, Santa Clara Pueblo.

Dona Tafoya. Pot not available.

Cookie Perez (portrait not available). Pot 1 ½ x 2 ¼ in., 1993. Rick Dillingham inventory.

Valerie Ochoa, b. 1974
"I've been doing it [pottery making] since I was about nine. I think it's important because it helps to keep the tradition of potters in our family alive. I do
simple little carved bowls, and some uncarved. I enjoy making them, you
have a reason to get dirty! I learned everything from my grandma [Mida
Tafoya]."

Mary Louise Eckleberry, b. 1921
"Since I was little, we [Mary Louise and her sisters] helped Mom [Christina
Naranjo] with the potteries. We made little ones, but they wanted to save their
clay. We lived in Indiana from 1946, and we returned here [Santa Clara] in
1982. After I came back to live here I started up again. Mom used to make
birds and turtles, so I make them also. The melon bowls—people were looking for it, and you just try to do it. I also do some wedding vases."

Victor Eckleberry, b. 1958, and Naomi Eckleberry, b. 1961
Naomi: "Victor does storage jars and 'eggs,' and I do wedding vases and
bowls."
[From a printout she gave me] "To create my pieces—inspiration, enthusiasm,
patience, and creativity come from within. My hands and a few simple tools
do the rest."

Victor [no photo]: "It's how I feed my kids. I work part-time on construction and
go fishing in the canyon. Life revolves around my work—almost every day.
It's art, but it's also a part of you. You're always thinking about it. It doesn't go
away. It's intense and not just a one-day thing. It's everything. Mixing the clay,
firing, there's a lot that goes into a final piece that people don't see."

Opposite: Valerie Ochoa. Pot not available.

Left: Mary Louise Eckleberry. Pot 2 ¾ x 3 ¾ in., ca. 1990. Courtesy of the artist.

Right: Victor Eckleberry (portrait not available). Pot 3 ½ x 2 ¾ in., 1992. Courtesy of the artist.

SAN ILDEFONSO

The Gonzales Family

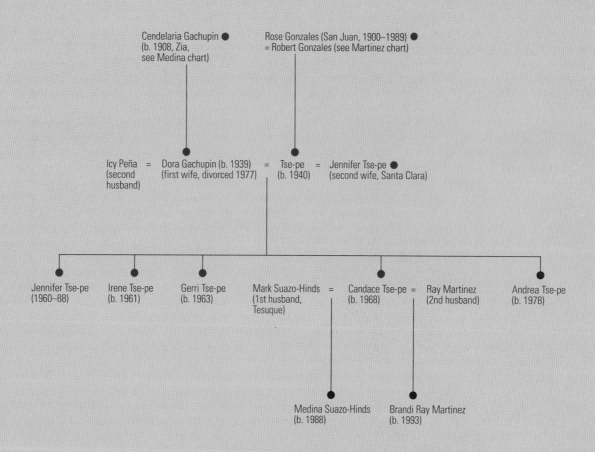

Cendelaria Gachupin ●
(b. 1908, Zia,
see Medina chart)

Rose Gonzales (San Juan, 1900–1989) ●
= Robert Gonzales (see Martinez chart)

Icy Peña   =   Dora Gachupin (b. 1939)   =   Tse-pe   =   Jennifer Tse-pe ●
(second   (first wife, divorced 1977)   (b. 1940)   (second wife, Santa Clara)
husband)

Jennifer Tse-pe
(1960–88)

Irene Tse-pe
(b. 1961)

Gerri Tse-pe
(b. 1963)

Mark Suazo-Hinds   =   Candace Tse-pe   =   Ray Martinez
(1st husband,   (b. 1968)   (2nd husband)
Tesuque)

Andrea Tse-pe
(b. 1978)

Medina Suazo-Hinds
(b. 1988)

Brandi Ray Martinez
(b. 1993)

Rose Gonzales, ca. 1973 (photo by Dick Dunatchik). Pots: previous page: red, 4 ½ x 9 in., ca. 1935, IAF 2089, courtesy Indian Arts Research Center, School of American Research, Santa Fe; black, 9 ½ x 10 ½ in., ca. 1975, courtesy Dora Tse-Pe Peña, San Ildefonso Pueblo.

Opposite: Tse-Pe. Pot 13 ¾ in. diameter, 1990. Rick Dillingham inventory.

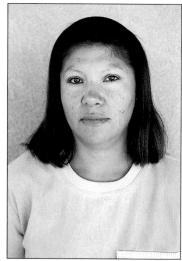

Tse-Pe, b. 1940
"With the changing of times, I'm finding still I have a strong urge in wanting to and continuing what Mother Earth has let me do—that is, her allowing me to make her as pretty as I can.

"I find myself feeling probably the strongest that I have felt in all these years I've been molding the beautiful clay. I have fun and different innovative feelings since I have started working with my wife, Jennifer. She in her own pottery-making right comes from a grandmother and mother who are accomplished potters [San Juan]. We try not to separate too much. We both gather clay and clean it, and after it's set [Mother Earth] takes some first, and we see what the mood sets up, who sits at the workbench first.

"We do all stages together: cleaning, making, polishing. I do the designs and she [Jennifer] helps, she's very much involved. We both fire together. The finishing we both do, adding stones and whatever. The end results are shared, we give a lot of thanks. My thoughts and my prayers and thankfulness have all been fulfilled and it all leads to my late mother Rose [Gonzales]. She was my inspiration, something that will never be forgotten. My everyday thanksgiving goes to those—and all who have been a part of me in the pottery world or anywhere."

Jennifer Tse-Pe, b. 1960
"In the past three years I would consider myself a potter. I saw my grandmother and mother doing it as I was growing up, but it was just a thing I saw. I saw them happy working and enjoying it. I didn't actually learn from them but experienced it growing up. It all fell into place, I didn't find it hard or a chore.

"I saw Tse-Pe enjoying it and working with it. It wasn't a chore. Somewhere there, Tse-Pe deserves a lot of credit, including [from] myself, who admire his work."

Tse-Pe.

Jennifer Tse-Pe. Pot not available.

Opposite: Candelaria Gachupin. Pot 7 1/2 x 11 1/2 in., ca. 1970. Courtesy Dora Tse-Pe Peña, San Ildefonso Pueblo.

Candelaria Gachupin, b. 1908
"I started since the 1930s and I'm still doing little pieces. I have some made, and I've always worked in traditional style. I use two backgrounds [slips] like her [referring to a photo of Rosalea Medina], and I do the same. I learned from Rosalea. My mother was a potter, but she passed away when I was a little girl. People asked her to make cooking pots because there wasn't the market there is now. They used them for serving dishes—there weren't so many store-bought dishes then. I taught Dora to do Zia style before she got married, then she started making black pottery after her mother-in-law, Rose [Gonzales].

Dora Tse-Pe Peña, b. 1939
Married in 1961 to Tse-Pe and divorced in 1977
"The most important thing [at Zia Pueblo], along
with working with my mother [Candelaria Gachu-
pin], was the way she taught me spirituality, the
sacredness of clay and respect for the clay. By
the time I started work here [San Ildefonso], I
already knew all that. I knew how to make pots,
and Grandma Rose [Gonzales] helped me to adapt
to the San Ildefonso clay. From her I learned to do
the polishing, which isn't done at Zia. I call what I
have a gift—it was almost an overnight success. In
1971 at Gallup [Inter-Tribal Ceremonial] I got a
Best of Class competing with the 'greats.' It was a
great inspiration.

"I hope and pray that my girls will continue with
their pots, and they learn all they can from me
while I'm here. I encourage them to do the carving,
like Grandma Rose and me. Not many are doing
the carving now. To me it's important to respect and
care for the pots. I don't make many. I would rather
work on quality than quantity."

Opposite: Dora Tse-Pe Peña. Pot 6 x 4
in., 1992. Rick Dillingham inventory.

Tse-Pe and Dora. Pot 4 ½ x 7 ¾ in.,
1972. Courtesy Adobe Gallery,
Albuquerque.

Irene Tse-Pe, b. 1961
"I feel fortunate to have grown up among good potters and pottery. My early memories of my grandmothers [Rose Gonzales and Candelaria Gachupin] have always been of them working with pottery. I was around Grandma Rose more. She was always so peaceful working on pots. I remember focusing on her hands, watching her work on pots. I want to carry on the carving tradition that Grandma Rose did. Some people say it's not real creative by not trying other things, but that's what I want to do."

Opposite: Irene Tse-Pe. Pot 3 ½ x 3 ¼ in., ca. 1987. Courtesy Dora Tse-Pe Peña, San Ildefonso Pueblo.

Candace Tse-Pe. Pot 2 ¼ x 2 ½ in., 1992. Courtesy of the artist.

The Martinez Family

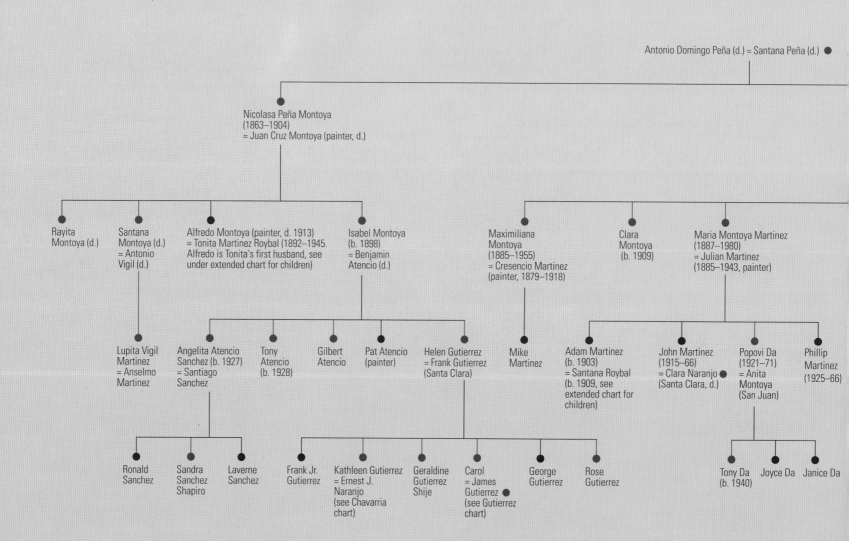

Antonio Domingo Peña (d.) = Santana Peña (d.)

Nicolasa Peña Montoya
(1863–1904)
= Juan Cruz Montoya (painter, d.)

Rayita
Montoya (d.)

Santana
Montoya (d.)
= Antonio
Vigil (d.)

Alfredo Montoya (painter, d. 1913)
= Tonita Martinez Roybal (1892–1945.
Alfredo is Tonita's first husband, see
under extended chart for children)

Isabel Montoya
(b. 1898)
= Benjamin
Atencio (d.)

Maximiliana
Montoya
(1885–1955)
= Cresencio Martinez
(painter, 1879–1918)

Clara
Montoya
(b. 1909)

Maria Montoya Martinez
(1887–1980)
= Julian Martinez
(1885–1943, painter)

Lupita Vigil
Martinez
= Anselmo
Martinez

Angelita Atencio
Sanchez (b. 1927)
= Santiago
Sanchez

Tony
Atencio
(b. 1928)

Gilbert
Atencio

Pat Atencio
(painter)

Helen Gutierrez
= Frank Gutierrez
(Santa Clara)

Mike
Martinez

Adam Martinez
(b. 1903)
= Santana Roybal
(b. 1909, see
extended chart for
children)

John Martinez
(1915–66)
= Clara Naranjo
(Santa Clara, d.)

Popovi Da
(1921–71)
= Anita
Montoya
(San Juan)

Phillip
Martinez
(1925–66)

Ronald
Sanchez

Sandra
Sanchez
Shapiro

Laverne
Sanchez

Frank Jr.
Gutierrez

Kathleen Gutierrez
= Ernest J.
Naranjo
(see Chavarria
chart)

Geraldine
Gutierrez
Shije

Carol
= James
Gutierrez
(see Gutierrez
chart)

George
Gutierrez

Rose
Gutierrez

Tony Da
(b. 1940)

Joyce Da

Janice Da

250

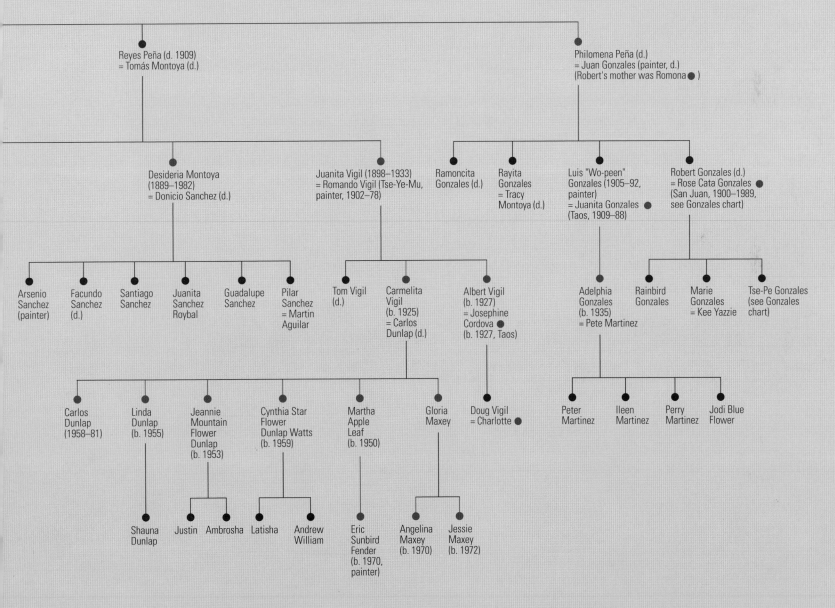

Reyes Peña (d. 1909)
= Tomás Montoya (d.)

Philomena Peña (d.)
= Juan Gonzales (painter, d.)
(Robert's mother was Romona ●)

Desideria Montoya
(1889–1982)
= Donicio Sanchez (d.)

Juanita Vigil (1898–1933)
= Romando Vigil (Tse-Ye-Mu,
painter, 1902–78)

Ramoncita
Gonzales (d.)

Rayita
Gonzales
= Tracy
Montoya (d.)

Luis "Wo-peen"
Gonzales (1905–92,
painter)
= Juanita Gonzales
(Taos, 1909–88)

Robert Gonzales (d.)
= Rose Cata Gonzales
(San Juan, 1900–1989,
see Gonzales chart)

Arsenio
Sanchez
(painter)

Facundo
Sanchez
(d.)

Santiago
Sanchez

Juanita
Sanchez
Roybal

Guadalupe
Sanchez

Pilar
Sanchez
= Martin
Aguilar

Tom Vigil
(d.)

Carmelita
Vigil
(b. 1925)
= Carlos
Dunlap (d.)

Albert Vigil
(b. 1927)
= Josephine
Cordova ●
(b. 1927, Taos)

Adelphia
Gonzales
(b. 1935)
= Pete Martinez

Rainbird
Gonzales

Marie
Gonzales
= Kee Yazzie

Tse-Pe Gonzales
(see Gonzales
chart)

Carlos
Dunlap
(1958–81)

Linda
Dunlap
(b. 1955)

Jeannie
Mountain
Flower
Dunlap
(b. 1953)

Cynthia Star
Flower
Dunlap Watts
(b. 1959)

Martha
Apple
Leaf
(b. 1950)

Gloria
Maxey

Doug Vigil
= Charlotte ●

Peter
Martinez

Ileen
Martinez

Perry
Martinez

Jodi Blue
Flower

Shauna
Dunlap

Justin

Ambrosha

Latisha

Andrew
William

Eric
Sunbird
Fender
(b. 1970,
painter)

Angelina
Maxey
(b. 1970)

Jessie
Maxey
(b. 1972)

The Martinez (extended) Family

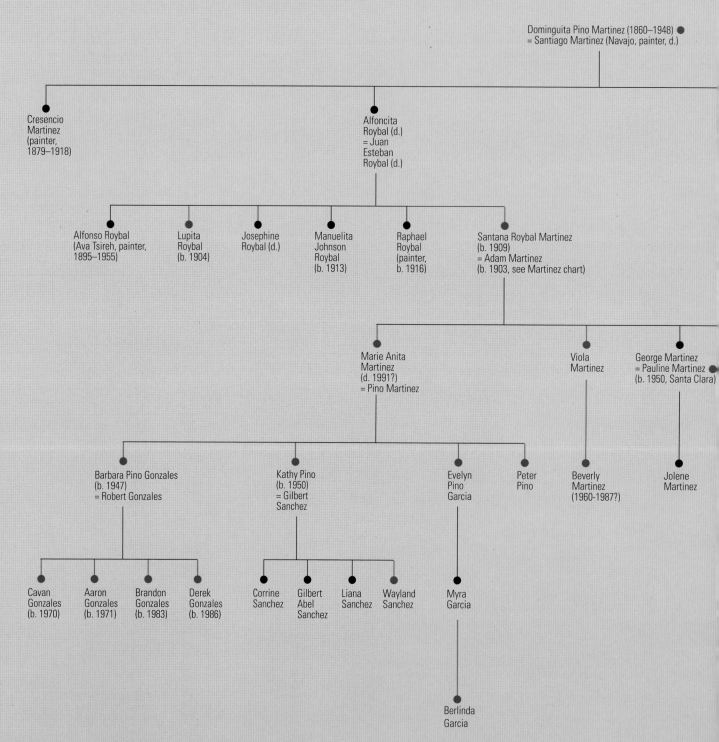

Dominguita Pino Martinez (1860–1948) ●
= Santiago Martinez (Navajo, painter, d.)

Cresencio Martinez (painter, 1879–1918)

Alfoncita Roybal (d.) = Juan Esteban Roybal (d.)

Alfonso Roybal (Ava Tsireh, painter, 1895–1955)

Lupita Roybal (b. 1904)

Josephine Roybal (d.)

Manuelita Johnson Roybal (b. 1913)

Raphael Roybal (painter, b. 1916)

Santana Roybal Martinez (b. 1909) = Adam Martinez (b. 1903, see Martinez chart)

Marie Anita Martinez (d. 1991?) = Pino Martinez

Viola Martinez

George Martinez = Pauline Martinez (b. 1950, Santa Clara)

Barbara Pino Gonzales (b. 1947) = Robert Gonzales

Kathy Pino (b. 1950) = Gilbert Sanchez

Evelyn Pino Garcia

Peter Pino

Beverly Martinez (1960-1987?)

Jolene Martinez

Cavan Gonzales (b. 1970)

Aaron Gonzales (b. 1971)

Brandon Gonzales (b. 1983)

Derek Gonzales (b. 1986)

Corrine Sanchez

Gilbert Abel Sanchez

Liana Sanchez

Wayland Sanchez

Myra Garcia

Berlinda Garcia

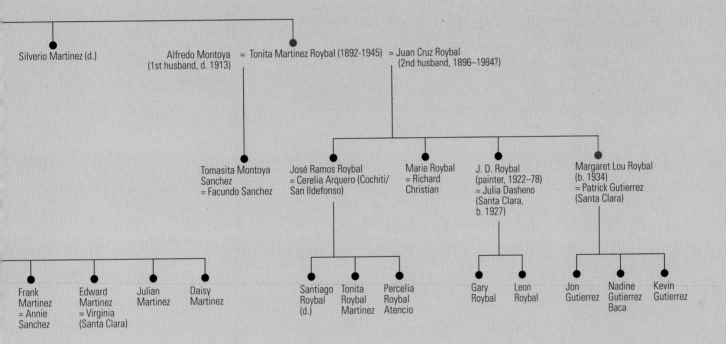

Silverio Martinez (d.)

Alfredo Montoya = Tonita Martinez Roybal (1892-1945) = Juan Cruz Roybal
(1st husband, d. 1913)   (2nd husband, 1896–1984?)

Tomasita Montoya
Sanchez
= Facundo Sanchez

José Ramos Roybal
= Cerelia Arquero (Cochiti/
San Ildefonso)

Marie Roybal
= Richard
Christian

J. D. Roybal
(painter, 1922–78)
= Julia Dasheno
(Santa Clara,
b. 1927)

Margaret Lou Roybal
(b. 1934)
= Patrick Gutierrez
(Santa Clara)

Frank
Martinez
= Annie
Sanchez

Edward
Martinez
= Virginia
(Santa Clara)

Julian
Martinez

Daisy
Martinez

Santiago
Roybal
(d.)

Tonita
Roybal
Martinez

Percelia
Roybal
Atencio

Gary
Roybal

Leon
Roybal

Jon
Gutierrez

Nadine
Gutierrez
Baca

Kevin
Gutierrez

Maximiliana Montoya (portrait not available). Black-on-black pot, 5 ½ x 6 ¾ in., ca. 1955. SAR 1988-6-80, courtesy Indian Arts Research Center, School of American Research, Santa Fe.

Top: Desideria Sanchez (with Maria Martinez), ca. 1973. Opposite: black-on-black pot, 6 x 9 ¼ in., ca. 1940. Courtesy Carmelita Dunlap.

Albert and Josephine Vigil
Josephine, b. 1927 (Taos)
"I didn't get to know her [Juanita Vigil], but from
our Aunt Maria [Martinez]. What we [Albert and
Josephine] do is cream-on-red pottery, and that's
our main work. I used to do black, and I saw Aunt
Maria doing some red and I decided to work more
with the red. I think it's over twenty years we've
been working on pots. I do all the work, and he
[Albert] does the painting. He painted before on
paper and let that go. Then he started with painting pottery.

"My mom [from Taos] used to do the mica pots
but never sold them. She made them for use. Her
work is a lot different than what we are doing
here. We were in L.A. for fifteen years, and when
we returned [to San Ildefonso] we made pottery
for a living. I used to watch Aunt Maria, and she
encouraged me to work with pottery. My husband
works, and he paints when he has time.

"I started learning polishing from Clara [Montoya].
She was the one—we used to get together and she
would teach me. I wanted to try the polychrome. I
noticed some of the red pottery is fired in kilns. We
do the open firing."

*Opposite: Albert Vigil and Josephine
Vigil. Pot 8 ¼ x 6 ¼ in., 1992. Courtesy Andrews Pueblo Pottery, Albuquerque.*

Carmelita Dunlap, b. 1925
My Aunt Maria and Desideria—I learned from them by just watching them.
They used to tell me to sit down and watch so I could learn. My mother
[Juanita Vigil] passed away when I was small—Maria and Desideria raised
us. We stay with the traditional ways—the black-on-black. I do polychrome,
too, the cream color, and I do red-on-black and brown ware, which is our
invention. Carlos found out about it.

"I learned a lot of things from Desideria and some things from Aunt Maria
too. I think they all used to work together, the sisters, and Desideria used to
work by herself. We called her Grandma. We would stay with Desideria for a
couple months, and then stay with Aunt Maria a couple months.

"I used to make real small ones and little animals. We returned from California
in the mid 1950s and I really started up with pottery."

258

Opposite: Carmelita Dunlap. Black-on-black pot, 4 ¼ x 7 ¾ in., 1992. Courtesy Merrock Galeria, Santa Clara Pueblo.

Carlos Dunlap, ca. 1978 (courtesy Carmelita Dunlap). Polychrome pot 3 x 13 in., ca. 1975. Courtesy Margaret Gutierrez.

Linda Dunlap, b. 1955
"I would say the same thing as my mother. What I'm doing is traditional pot-tery, and I learned from Mom and Carlos. We all have different shapes we do. I'm trying to make bigger ones, but I usually work in smaller sizes. I learned the making mostly from my mom, and with Carlos I learned about painting and firing. I want to keep on and see how far I can take it. I have a daughter and will help her with it."

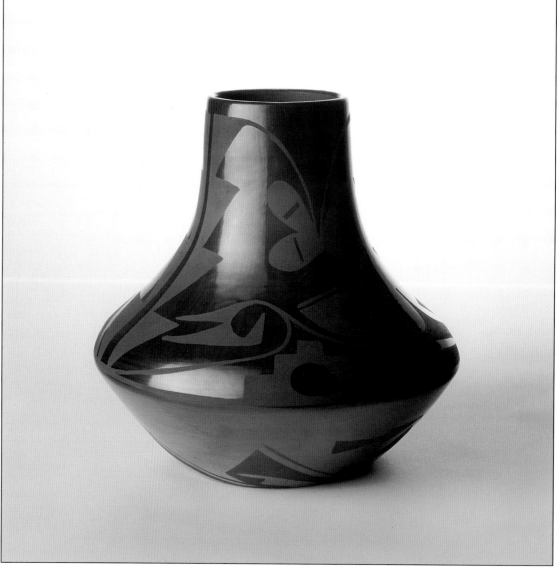

Jeannie Mountain Flower Dunlap, b. 1953
"I'm following in my mom's [Carmelita Dunlap's] footsteps, and I'm helping her when I can with her work. Ever since Carlos died, I've been helping her. Linda [Dunlap], Mom, and I fire our pots and work together here at the house. It was hard for her to do the big pots, so I started helping her."

Cynthia Star Flower Dunlap Watts, b. 1959
"On my work I try to take my time and not rush, because if you rush they don't come out good. I used to watch Carmelita and Carlos [Dunlap]. They would encourage me. I started with little ones and got to larger ones. I do all my work myself.

"I live in Cortez [Colorado], and I work there. My husband started encouraging me more after I moved to Colorado. He encouraged me to keep it up. He's making buffalos and bears, and my daughter Latisha makes small ones, and my son Andrew makes and paints his pots.

"Everybody likes my polishing and painting. It's coming out a lot better now than before. My mom made me do it and keep trying."

Opposite: Linda Dunlap. Pot 8 ½ x 8 in., 1991. Courtesy of the artist.

Jeannie Mountain Flower Dunlap. Pot not available.

Cynthia Star Flower Dunlap Watts. Pot 18 x 11 ½ in., 1992. Courtesy of the artist.

Martha Apple Leaf Fender, b. 1950
"[My main influences were] Maria and Desideria, I remember I grew up with her [Desideria] and later I worked with Carlos. I learned how to really make them [pottery] from him. He would help make them for us and then he would smash them down and get us to make them ourselves. I enjoy the black and also do green on red, it's different—but I haven't worked on those lately. It was supposed to be white like Uncle Albert [Vigil] but it cooled to green. I got the color from Uncle Tse-Pe. I like working with it— it's something new. Erik [Fender] learned from my mom and I and now he does most of the painting for me—so much easier."

Erik Sunbird Fender (Than Tsideh), b. 1970
"When I got into doing the pottery, it was from watching Grandmother [Carmelita Dunlap], Mom [Martha], and Uncle Carlos. I guess it just rubbed off on me. I got into experimenting with different kinds of clay and firing techniques, and from there I developed my styles now. [My preference is] between black-on-black, polychrome, and black-on-red. There's nobody here at the pueblo who does black-on-red—it's a lost technique. I'm trying to revive it in a way, I guess. Now I'm looking at old photos of pots and I get inspiration from them . . . especially my shapes now. I love to look at old polychrome pieces for ideas."

Opposite left: Martha Apple Leaf (portrait not available). Pot 4 ⅜ x 5 ¾ in., 1992. Courtesy Merrock Galeria, Santa Clara Pueblo.

Opposite right: Erik Sunbird Fender (Than Tsideh). Pot 2 x 11 ¾ in., 1991. Courtesy of the artist and Carmelita Dunlap.

Maria Martinez, ca. 1973. Pots: black, signed "Marie," 5 x 8 ½ in., ca. 1925, IAF 1889, courtesy Indian Arts Research Center, School of American Research, Santa Fe; opposite: red carved, signed "Marie and Julian," 6 x 7 in., ca. 1925–30, Rick Dillingham collection.

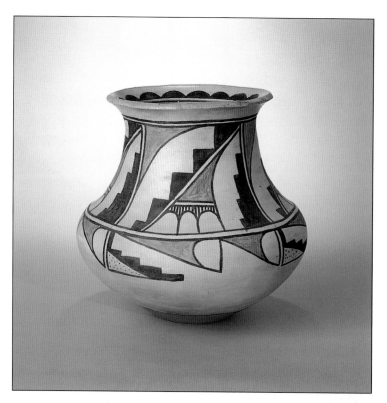

Maria Martinez. Pots: top: Marie and Julian polychrome, unsigned, 10 x 10 ½ in., ca. 1915–20, IAF 2637, courtesy Indian Arts Research Center, School of American Research, Santa Fe; bottom: Marie and Julian polychrome plaque, signed "Marie," 10 in. diameter, ca. 1920–25, courtesy Buckner/Lazarus collection, New York; opposite: black-on-black, signed "Marie and Julian," ca. 1940, 7 x 9 in., Rick Dillingham inventory.

Maria Martinez. Pots: opposite: black with no design, signed "Marie and Santana," 3 ½ x 13 ¾ in., ca. 1950, IAF 2819, courtesy Indian Arts Research Center, School of American Research, Santa Fe; top: plain black-ware, signed "Maria Poveka," 6 x 13 in., April, 1967 ("467"), IAF 3129, courtesy Indian Arts Research Center, School of American Research, Santa Fe; bottom: black-on-black, signed "Maria and Popovi," plate 2 x 11 ¼ in., October 1970 ("1070"), Rick Dillingham collection.

Popovi Da and Maria Martinez, ca. 1960 (photograph by Maurice Eby, courtesy Anita M. Da). Pots: black-on-black, 4 x 5 in., March 1971 ("371"), courtesy Buckner/Lazarus collection, New York; opposite: made by Maria Martinez and finished by Popovi Da and Tony Da, 2 ¼ x 7 ½ in., June 1970 ("670"), courtesy Buckner/Lazarus collection, New York.

Tony Da, ca. 1970 (photograph by Laura Gilpin, courtesy Anita M. Da). Opposite: redware pot, 7 x 7 in., ca. 1970–72, Rick Dillingham inventory; bear figure, 3 x 5 ½ in. long, ca. 1968, courtesy Anita M. Da.

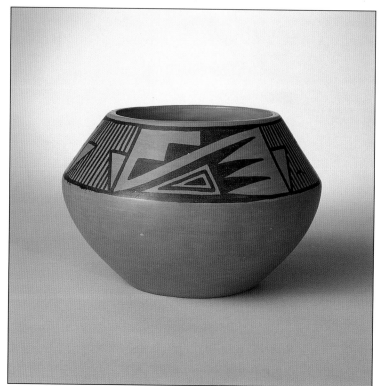

Tonita Roybal and Juan Cruz Roybal.
Pots: left: white and red-on-red, ca.
1925, 7 ¾ x 9 ¼ in., IAF 2087, courtesy Indian Arts Research Center,
School of American Research, Santa
Fe; right: black-on-red, ca. 1923, 6 x
8 ½ in., Rick Dillingham inventory.

Opposite: Dominguita Pino (mother)
and Tonita Roybal, 11 ½ x 12 ½ in., ca.
1910–14. Rick Dillingham collection.

Santana Martinez, b. 1909
"I like my work, but I'm taking it kind of easy. I can't do too much. Right now I'm trying to finish some small pots. I feel very happy about the young children doing the work, and I'm trying to help them. They're doing pretty good.

"I feel I was lucky to have Maria and Julian help me—Maria with my pots, and Julian with decoration. I have my own family—my mother, grandmother, and aunt—who were also potters. I have only one daughter, Anita, working.

"Clara [Montoya] still polishes for us, but she won't polish the big pieces anymore.

"When I started decorating, I signed Marie and Santana, and then I started just signing my name, not with Adam then. Some white people were here and said they had seen one of my pots in a grocery store—it was a Santo Domingo pot with 'Santana' on it. That's when we started signing Santana and Adam."

Santana and Adam Martinez (portrait of Santana only). Opposite: pot 5 ½ x 5 ½ in., 1979. Rick Dillingham collection.

Margaret Lou Gutierrez, b. 1934.
"My dad [Juan Cruz Roybal] was my main teacher.
He wanted me to try and make pottery like they
did when mother [Tonita Roybal] was still living.
He encouraged the black-on-black. My dad said,
'Stick to traditional,' and I always did. I've tried the
red [pottery], but I like the black. He [Juan Cruz
Roybal] taught me how to paint different styles of
designs that he used to make, also J. D. Roybal
helped me with painting.

"I moved to Santa Clara in 1957 when I got married. I started potting in around 1971–72. I was still
small, I was ten when she [Tonita Roybal] died. I
remember going to Indian Market when they had
it under the portal. I remember her making pottery
and my dad painting.

"My favorite style is the feather design from San
Ildefonso. I came across some of my mother's pottery and a lot of people tell me they [my pots]
resemble her pots a lot."

*Opposite: Tonita Roybal and Juan
Cruz Roybal. Pot black-on-black, ca.
1930–35, 8 ½ x 8 in., IAF 2091,
courtesy Indian Arts Research Center, School of American Research,
Santa Fe.*

*Margaret Lou Gutierrez. Pot painted
by Elvis Torres. Courtesy Torres
Indian Arts, San Ildefonso Pueblo.*

Opposite: Marie Anita Martinez
(d. 1992) (portrait not available). Pot
6 x 5 in., 1991. Courtesy Anita M. Da.

Barbara Gonzales (Tahn-Moo-Whe).
Pot 2 x 4 in., 1980. Courtesy Andrews
Pueblo Pottery, Albuquerque.

Cavan Gonzalez, b. 1970
"I just got my B.F.A. from Alfred University in upstate New York. I went to school there to get a different approach to the art world rather than staying in the Southwest and being taught what everyone else already knew. I want to go on for my M.F.A., and my future is to teach college-level intaglio and/or ceramics. I'm having fun with etchings, zinc plate, and woodcuts. Now I'm experimenting with polychrome pottery. It seems like a lost or forgotten tradition. It was traditional before black pots."

 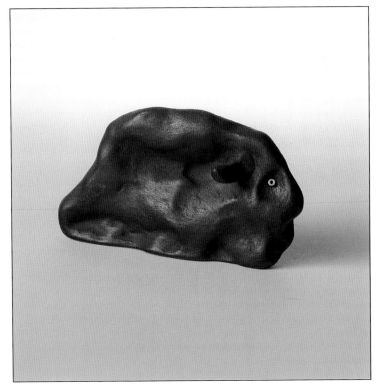

*Opposite: Cavan Gonzales. Pot 3 x
11 ¾ in., 1992. Courtesy Dewey
Galleries, Ltd., Santa Fe.*

*Left: Derek Gonzales. Figure 1 ⅛ x
2 ¼ in., 1992. Courtesy Pat Lollar.*

*Right: Brandon Gonzales. Figure
2 ¼ x 4 in., 1992. Courtesy Pat Lollar.*

Pauline Martinez, b. 1950
"I am from Santa Clara and did pottery with my mother [Crecencia Tafoya].
When I married George Martinez in 1970, I moved to San Ildefonso. I continued
to work with my mom. I began to work with Santana [Martinez], and she used
to paint for me. Clara [Montoya] helped polish the bigger ones and did the
small ones.

"I've stayed with traditional feathers and avanyu designs. I do wedding vases,
melon bowls, and black-on-black pottery. I'll probably continue what I'm doing
now and hopefully will do bigger pots. I'm doing my own painting now."

Kathy Sanchez, b. 1950
"I think pottery making is a very important pathway to relate to the earth.
The earth is the one that nurtures you, and you want to relate to it, acknowl-
edge its importance in your life, acknowledge it every day. Working with clay
reminds you of the connectedness of everything. I was married in 1970 and
began potting then, also after I finished college.

"You learn all of life's messages from the pathway of working with clay. I like
to relate to the spiritual side. Pottery has become so commercial, you tend to be
physically oriented rather than spiritually oriented. It's easy to loose focus."

Opposite left: Pauline Martinez. Pot
3 ¼ x 3 ½ in., 1990. Rick Dillingham
inventory.

Opposite right: Kathy Sanchez (por-
trait not available). Bear fetish:
height 4 in., 1992. Courtesy Torres
Indian Arts, San Ildefonso.

Isabel Montoya Atencio. (portrait not
available). Pot 6 x 8 in.,ca. 1965.
Courtesy Gilbert Atencio.

Adelphia Martinez, b. 1935
"My influences would be from my mother after she came down from Taos. She did some black and red [pottery] with my aunt, Rose Gonzales. The other influence was my father. He was a watercolor artist. He did horses and dancers. He always encouraged us to do our best. My Taos grandmother did the micaceous pottery and I use some mica in my work and incorporate Taos and San Ildefonso. I do sgraffito and carving and work both in black and red. My mom and Aunt Rose did a lot of carving and I learned from them. Their styles were similiar and I've been told mine looks like theirs."

Opposite: Juanita Gonzales and "Wo-peen" Gonzales. Plate 7 ½ in. diameter, ca. 1955. Courtesy Andrew Fisher Fine Pottery, Santa Fe.

Adelphia Martinez. Wedding vase 9 x 6 in., 1993. Courtesy of the artist.

Opposite: Gilbert Atencio. Plate 10
in. diameter, ca. 1980. Courtesy of
the artist.

Left: Helen Gutierrez. Plate 10 in.
diameter, ca. 1988. Courtesy Torres
Indian Arts, San Ildefonso Pueblo.

Right: Romona Gonzales (portrait not
available). Pseudo-ceremonial box
5 x 6 ¾ in., ca. 1930.